The

THIRD
EDITION

Classroom
Observer

Developing
Observation Skills
in Early Childhood
Settings

The Classroom Observer

THIRD
EDITION

Developing Observation Skills in Early Childhood Settings

Ann E. Boehm
Richard A. Weinberg

FOREWORD BY
JEANNE BROOKS-GUNN

TEACHERS
COLLEGE
PRESS

Teachers College
Columbia University
New York and London

The first edition of this book appeared in 1977 under the title, *The Classroom Observer: A Guide for Developing Observational Skills.*

Text photographs by Myron Papiz and Nancy Johnson

Published by Teachers College Press, 1234 Amsterdam Avenue, New York, NY 10027

Library of Congress Cataloging-in-Publication Data

Boehm, Ann E., 1938–
    The classroom observer : developing observation skills in early
childhood settings / Ann E. Boehm and Richard A. Weinberg ; foreword
by Jeanne Brooks-Gunn ; [text photographs by Myron Papiz and Nancy
Johnson].—3rd ed.
        p.   cm
    Includes bibliographical references and index.
    ISBN 0-8077-3570-1 (pbk. : alk. paper)
    1. Observation (Educational method) 2. Child development.
3. Early childhood education.   I. Weinberg, Richard A.   II. Title.
LB1027.28.B64   1997
371.3'9—dc20   96-28688

ISBN 0-8077-3570-1 (paper)

Printed on acid-free paper
Manufactured in the United States of America

04 03 02 01 00 99 98 97   8 7 6 5 4 3 2 1

To
Gail and Neville,
again

Contents

List of Tasks

Foreword

It is a great pleasure to have this third edition of *The Classroom Observer: Developing Observation Skills in Early Childhood Settings*. The authors, Ann Boehm and Richard Weinberg, have, in keeping with their earlier editions, written a thoughtful and much-needed volume on observing children. They have updated previous versions by adding more information on the usefulness of observational techniques for practitioners, for trainers of early childhood education teachers, and for students. They always keep their eye on the prize—in this case, providing a framework, or set of frameworks, in which to observe children and to evaluate the information gleaned from such observations. Boehm and Weinberg speak to educators, both as empiricists and as ethnographers—the key to successful pedagogy is listening to, watching, and interacting with students. No amount of training in specific curriculum approaches can replace good observation skills *and* the integration of lessons learned from watching children in everyday classroom activities.

The Classroom Observer provides the foundation for learning how to watch children in systematic and child-focused ways. The authors make the critical and often underappreciated point that keen insight into children's development may be learned, and that while many early childhood educators already watch children, much can be gained from systematic observation. I believe that this book provides a basis for critical reflection upon one's own observation skills. The information also gives much needed tips, and exercises, to move educators to develop a procedure for adding to, or even altering, the ways in which they use informal observations when interacting with children. The ability to reflect upon one's interpretation of observations, and then to alter them, is at the crux of the authors' work.

Their learner-oriented approach applies not only to how we interact with children, but how we learn as educators (here, I include all those who work with and enjoy young children as educators—family care providers, teacher aides, nurses, social workers, family life counselors, home visitors, and parents, as well as teachers). By writing about observation in such an engaging and interactive way, *The Classroom Observer* is fun as well as informative.

The authors also provide a service by focusing on a number of thorny, and perennial, observational problems. These are issues from which all of us watching children grow up cannot escape, even after years of engaging children in classrooms, on playgrounds, in our own homes, or in our research laboratories. Perhaps the most perplexing concern is how to watch groups of children. After all, schools, child care centers, and even homes have more than one child. The interactions among children provide the only window onto how children are adapting to a particular setting and when they are having difficulties with their classmates, siblings, or friends. Indeed, there is no substitute method for assessing social and emotional well-being in children other than watching them interact. *The Classroom Observer* provides great illustrations on group functioning.

A related but no less perplexing issue is how to interpret the behavior of children in different settings and from different backgrounds. Children's behavior does not occur in a vacuum. What we see, and what children allow us to see, is influenced by family and neighborhoods. In fact, I maintain that we will not understand children's development without placing it in context. I often talk about "children in families in communities," or at least believe that the term "children" is a shorthand for this longer phrase. The authors place children's behavior into context, and do so in a sensitive way. They make the important point that observers are often hampered by their own life view, or upbringing, in the ways in which they interpret a child's or a group of children's behavior. Part of the critical self-reflection needed by educators is that their worlds may be quite different from those of their children. Sensitivity to diversity, and the ability not to pre-judge a set of behaviors, is critical.

In conclusion, *The Classroom Observer* is a terrific volume. It is an honor to write the Foreword for it. I use the volume when teaching advanced undergraduate and master's students; all of us have learned from working with this volume. And, I hope that you will also profit from enhancing your own observation skills by watching children more closely and more critically, and by reflecting on the ways that you previously "listened" to what children's behavior was telling you.

Jeanne Brooks-Gunn

Preface—Third Edition

Historically, naturalistic observational techniques have been central to the development of the physical sciences, helping to generate theories and establish knowledge about physical phenomena. Rooted in the rich tradition of the physical sciences, the social sciences have opened our window of understanding about the social world through the use of systematic observational methods. Skill in observing children has been a cornerstone of the work of "child watchers," those professionals devoted to child study and to understanding why children develop and behave in the ways they do. Appreciating this heritage, we have developed a third, updated edition of *The Classroom Observer: Developing Observation Skills in Early Childhood Settings*. The program presented in this third edition focuses on the skills needed for an early childhood observer to make appropriate, valid inferences and to arrive at decisions based on objective observation data that can be gathered in natural learning habitats and educational settings. This book is based on the premise that observation skills are an indispensable component of an early childhood educator's professional repertoire. Educators are applied empiricists, and are therefore most effective when they have access to sound data to support their planning, interventions, and follow-up efforts.

Although observation is recognized as an important tool for gaining information, drawing conclusions, and generating ideas, limited attention has been devoted to many of the key issues surrounding the effective application of systematic observation in learning environments. *The aim of this book is to present critical components that must be considered in developing systematic observation skills when working in early childhood settings.* A major focus is also placed on *self-made* observation strategies rather than on "canned" products. To accomplish these goals, the reader is asked to engage in a series of tasks to develop an understanding of the various principles and procedures introduced. Sample responses are provided for many of these tasks in the Appendix, so that the reader can compare his or her answers with those of others.

The increasing availability of observation techniques for various professionals involved in the early childhood educational enterprise does not guarantee the development and assimilation of observation skills in training programs for teachers, special educators, health educators, school psychologists, social workers, and other school personnel devoted to the welfare of young children.

Observing children in educational contexts and preparing case studies have been integral components of the training of some individuals engaged in preschool and elementary education. However, our experience in directing in-service workshops for child care providers, practicing teachers, special educators, and school psychologists has indicated that a step-by-step program for developing objective observation skills is essential if adequate naturalistic observation techniques are to be acquired. Such programs can be incorporated into teacher and other professional training programs as well as in-service and continuing education opportunities. Field experiences and observation practice supplementary to traditional course work and student–teacher experiences can generate interesting seminar discussions about the role of observation in the early childhood education process. The adjunct use of videotaped classroom scenes can provide exercises in studying such concepts as observer reliability, the procedures for generating categories of behavior, and the strategies that children use to solve problems.

Multidisciplinary workshops (involving team teachers, student teachers, classroom paraprofessionals, and supportive pupil personnel such as school social workers and psychologists) that explore observational techniques can stress the value of a "team" approach to observing early childhood settings. By sharing their observational data, early childhood personnel can facilitate optimal educational programming. It should become obvious that by extending observational training to educational programs for effective parenting, one can generalize the value of systematic observation skills to the home and family situations. Furthermore, introducing parent observers to the classroom and other early childhood settings might stimulate communication about young children. Older students, too, can be productive observers who might benefit by training in systematic observation.

This third edition is an expanded and updated volume that maintains its focus on systematic observational skills building in early childhood environments. This edition includes expanded units on:

1. Detail of procedures for observing environmental factors that affect learning and behavior, and an overview of environmental scales appropriate to the instructional environment
2. The importance of observers' understanding the cultural and linguistic characteristics of children's learning environments
3. The key role of observation in the assessment process, includ-

ing the emerging role of assessment procedures used in the classroom such as curriculum-based assessment
4. The forms of observation with illustrative examples
5. The exploration of reliability, sampling behavior, recording formats, summarizing observational outcomes, and validity

A number of self-checks complement the exercise tasks to enhance the reader's skill-building. Expanded references and resources have also been incorporated. In addition to original photographs by Myron Papiz included in the first two editions, new photos taken at the University of Minnesota's Shirley G. Moore Laboratory School by Nancy Johnson have been included.

Although the primary target of our book is the community of professionals who study young children, the audience of educators, researchers, and human service providers who work with older populations should find this a useful addition to their resources.

The development of three editions of this volume has been a rewarding experience. We are especially appreciative of Millie Almy, who provided us with the initial impetus to write the book. Since the first edition was published, Byron Egeland, Erna Fishhaut, Lynn Galle, and Shirley Moore of the University of Minnesota's Institute of Child Development, and Margaret Jo Shepherd and Leslie R. Williams of Teachers College, Columbia University, provided us support and encouragement. John Swayze helped in important ways in the development of Unit X. Special thanks to Jeanne Brooks-Gunn for her Foreword to this edition. We also appreciate the suggestions and feedback from the students and teachers who employed earlier editions in their studies, the clerical assistance of Jeanette Yee, and the contributions of Susan Liddicoat and Karl Nyberg at Teachers College Press for shepherding this edition to publication. Finally, we offer thanks to the hundreds of young children in many learning settings whom we have observed and from whom we have learned.

Ann E. Boehm
Richard A. Weinberg
1996

The Classroom Observer

THIRD
EDITION

Developing
Observation Skills
in Early Childhood
Settings

An Introduction to the Skills of Observation

Today's world demands that each of us make judgments, evaluate situations, and guide our lives on the basis of inference. Many of these decisions and judgments are based on information that we derive from the environment through observation. We make observations in a variety of settings where we view people behaving in different ways. In our daily observations we take account of the interactions between individuals, the outcomes of interactions, the physical setting in which the exchanges occur, and the nature of the tasks involved. In these various situations the observation process allows us to obtain essential information for drawing inferences and making decisions, unfortunately with varying degrees of validity. We do this in mundane situations, such as inferring that a roast is finished when the meat thermometer registers "rare roast beef" (if we care for rare meat). The observation process also operates in more consequential areas of our lives:

- The coach critically reviews the videotape of the last basketball game and makes a decision as to which team members will start in the next game.
- The preschool teacher observes over a 2-week period the play patterns of her pupils to evaluate the nature of the interactions among children.
- The gymnast watches another competitor compete on the balance beam, observes components of performance not seen by the untrained eye, and makes a list of self-improvement points on which to work during practice.
- The radiologist "reads" a CAT scan for the surgeon, who in turn uses the data as well as the patient's medical history to determine the appropriate surgical technique.
- The birdwatcher, the artist, the meteorologist, the farmer, the coin collector, all observe the world through their unique lenses and guide their behavior, decisions, and judgments accordingly.

The level of precision with which one observes events is determined by one's interest, needs, and past experience. Much of what we see or do not see is the result of casual, nondirected activity. Systematic, scientific observation, however, requires guided observing of consistently observable events.

OBSERVING IN THE EARLY CHILDHOOD ARENA

The early childhood enterprise—educational and child care programs for young children and their families—has long been an arena of debate for parents, educators, behavioral scientists, politicians, and other groups with vested interests in the welfare of young children. Controversy focuses on children's needs, effective strategies for accomplishing educational and developmental goals for individual children, the advantages of varying programs and curricula, and alternative systems for providing services. Furthermore, conflicting political, economic, and social pressures confound the issues. In this climate of unrest and controversy, early childhood professionals, including teachers, administrators, and other specialists, must be all the more deliberate and objective as they go about their business of making inferences, solving daily problems, facilitating the educational process, and generally being accountable for their activities.

New students of observation skills often underestimate the complexities of systematic observation and fail to tap the rich information that is present when viewing a learning situation. For example, an untrained observer entering a kindergarten to observe the "classroom climate" might generate a 5-minute "running record" such as:

Boy crying in block corner.
Another child angry with his friend who has knocked over his block fort.
Teacher is ignoring both of these children while a male aide is attempting to intervene in both situations.
Room seems crowded.
Art materials are not being used.
Girls in housekeeping corner are involved in play.

Another observer trained in a systematic approach to making observations would generate a different 5-minute "running record" of the same situation: Given the purpose of "observing the classroom climate," the trained observer would develop a simple strategy for observing those components of the setting and child and teacher behavior that he or she defines ahead of time as components of a "classroom climate." The trained observer systematically takes account of each component by sampling from the situation over the given time period. Such a record might look like this:

Setting and people
There are 15 children present (7 girls, 8 boys).
The female teacher is assisted by one male (perhaps a student teacher).
The room is arranged in a variety of activity areas: painting area, doll corner, water table, block area, book area.

Pupil and teacher behavior
The presence of eight semi-dry paintings hanging on a clothesline suggests that the children were painting earlier.
There are at least two children participating in each of four activity areas (excluding painting).
The teacher is at her desk involved in some "paper activity."
The male (student teacher?) is speaking to the child who is crying in the block area.

Although there is overlap in the "running records" of both the untrained and trained observers, it should be evident that the more systematic approach will permit a stronger basis for arriving at inferences about "the classroom climate" of this particular kindergarten. Specifically, one can note that:

- The first running record, by confusing observations with inferences, gives the reader the impression that the overall classroom atmosphere is "unhappy." The second report indicates that the atmosphere is "busy" with an isolated "unhappy" incident.
- The second, more systematic report, supplies more factual information about the people and the setting.
- The first record simply misrepresents the degree of art activity in the room; the second, by taking account of additional information, gives a more valid report.

Thus, although both records provide descriptions of classroom climate, the second, more systematic, running record provides us with a more valid representation of the setting.

OBSERVING SYSTEMATICALLY

It is the purpose of this book to provide a systematic approach for observing in learning environments, especially those for young children. The observer, by developing simple observation skills and greater awareness of the valuable tool of observation, can approach the work knowing that decisions and conclusions have been based on a strong foundation of observation information.

Like the astute political and economic observer, the child observer must be aware of the distorting influences of subjective feelings and intuitive reactions on the observation process. Individuals frequently perceive the same situation differently, their observations reflecting their developmental level, cultural background, previous experiences, comprehension and understanding of the specific instance, and personal biases. Typical observations tend to reflect individual and egocentric frames of reference, which in turn mirror societal or cultural norms and/or prejudices. A few examples may help to underscore this point:

Individual perceptions
One person reading the *Wall Street Journal* notes, "This paper is dull and uninteresting." However, another person might state that "reading the *Wall Street Journal* provides stimulating information as to the current financial scene."

Cultural norms
A child looks at the floor when he is being taken to task by a teacher. To the child, as a result of his past experiences, this is an indication of deference to and respect for authority. From the standpoint of the teacher, such behavior may be viewed as deviousness, avoidance of confrontation, or admission of guilt.

Developmental influences
The work of Piaget has focused awareness on the fact that, up to about the age of 6 or 7, children believe all others perceive the world as they do. For example, from an egocentric frame of reference, a child might state that another person, irrespective of his or her position in the room, sees exactly the same things he or she does even if the objects are out of view of the other person.

Approaching a situation, the trained observer uses a systematic strategy for collecting information from the setting. What the observer focuses on and the pattern of observations that results are not random but are guided by the question posed or the problem needing to be solved.

The categories devised for labeling components of the setting, specific people in the observed situation, and behavioral activities that occur are precise and clearly defined.

In collecting and recording observations, the trained observer uses a system that allows a sampling of the situation, taking into account sources of bias. Through a sufficient number of objective observations, he or she is prepared to build valid inferences from a reliable, rich data base of direct observations in natural settings.

Our description of the trained early childhood observer summarizes the various observation skills that this book attempts to foster. The adage "seeing is believing" reflects the powerful role that observation plays in our lives, but it underestimates the advantages that the trained observer has over the naive observer.

In this book the key features of skilled observation are detailed, including defining the observation question and setting, labeling and categorizing observations, sampling and recording observations over time, and making reliable and valid observations. Exercises with feedback are provided to help classroom observers refine their skills.

Applying Observation Skills to Learning Settings

The program presented in this book is an attempt to demonstrate the role that systematic observation skills can play in one's daily decision-making activities. While we focus on early childhood settings and the observation of young children, observation procedures can be used to collect information throughout the educational spectrum, and we have drawn on examples from other educational settings and contexts. This unit provides a brief overview of the role observation methods have played in the study of children's behavior, the educational process, and classroom techniques. It also provides a perspective on how observation techniques can contribute to the efficiency of the teacher, psychologist, special educator, and other personnel involved in education.

OBSERVATION AS A METHOD OF INQUIRY

Historically, objective observation techniques have been central to the scientist's methods of inquiry for generating hypotheses, for building laws of science, and for confirming theories. However, such techniques were not always without difficulty. In fact, Galileo Galilei (1564–1642), the founder of modern astronomy, was condemned by the Church for his use of scientific observation. Having built an astronomical telescope and studied moving bodies in space, he noted that the earth orbited the sun, contrary to the accepted position that the earth was the center of the universe. In this instance, objective data came into direct conflict with a traditional belief that was difficult to refute.

The social sciences, rooted in the tradition of the physical and biological sciences, have also enlarged the scope of human knowledge by deriving conclusions based on objective, observable data. Often, this concern has been limited to the controlled situation of the experimenter's laboratory or the contrived situation of the researcher using questionnaires, rating scales, and clinical testing techniques where observations are made of the effects of an experimenter's manipulations.

The traditional experimental approach emphasizes an artificially controlled manipulation of the environment in order to gain knowledge of various phenomena (e.g., laboratory research in cancer treatment, the study of paired-associate learning behavior of children, the influences of a new curriculum on a child's mastery of a particular subject). The questions raised by the experimenters are these: If we alter the experimental situation in a particular way, what behaviors will result? How will these behaviors compare with those that occur when a different set of environmental conditions is presented? We often forget that observations of our natural "unaltered" environments provide the impetus for laboratory research and stimulate the development of hypotheses, speculations, and researchable ideas. On the other hand, empirical findings in the laboratory often must be verified in naturalistic settings before these results can be accepted.

In contrast, the ecological approach to studying phenomena emphasizes the investigation of observable phenomena as they occur naturally in the environment, uncontrolled by the observer. Sociologists and anthropologists (e.g., Mead, 1932; Parsons & Bales, 1955) have collected field data and used their observational findings in developing much of our understanding about social organizations, the influences of cultural factors on behavior, and the nature of daily living patterns in various groups. Psychologists have increasingly focused on the ecology of the individual and its environment by exploring behavior in the natural settings of the home, community, or classroom (e.g., Barker, 1968; Barker & Schoggen, 1973; Bronfenbrenner, 1977, 1979).

The valuable work of Barker and Wright at the Kansas Midwest Station has provided a wealth of information, unveiling the natural habitats and behaviors of individuals. *One Boy's Day: A Specimen Record of Behavior* (1951) and *Midwest and Its Children: The Psychological Ecology of an American Town* (1955) are classic works illustrating how a descriptive, naturalistic, ecological approach can contribute to our understanding of complex, ongoing human behavior in real-life situations, not laboratories. These works have also shown how an observer can accurately record a broad range of natural behavior through the use of specimen records. These in turn generate dimensions of behavior that can be further investigated through the use of other research techniques. Barker and Schoggen (1973) further resolved some conceptual and measurement problems central to studying environments and understanding the links between habitat and behavior. Such understanding enhances our ability to control or predict behavior and to improve the nature and quality of life.

OBSERVATION TECHNIQUES IN STUDYING CHILD DEVELOPMENT

The earliest systematic observations of children's behavior in natural settings were biographies, diaries, and detailed recordings of children's behavior. One can trace the practice of making diary descriptions or sequential accounts of ongoing activity to the late 18th century when many observers kept diaries tracing their children's development. For example, the Swiss educator Johann Pestalozzi (1746–1827) made extensive observations and kept records of the development of his 3½-year-old son. Other "baby biographies" appeared in the early 1900s, each providing an account of the observed development of a child who was a relative of the biographer. Although these biographies were of value in raising hypotheses about the nature of child development, their generalizability was limited. In addition, the observations were often unsystematic, biased, and selective (Scarr, Weinberg, & Levine, 1986). However, the detailed recordings of observations of children by Jean Piaget (1960), who charted our understanding of the cognitive development of children, and by Roger Brown (1973), who explored the acquisition of language— to cite two well-known examples—were critical underpinnings of the contemporary study of human development. The burgeoning study of human development across the life span from infancy through adulthood in the cognitive, perceptual-motor, social, and emotional domains is built on the work of these pioneer "child watchers."

Since the early 1970s, there has been an upsurge of interest among developmentalists in extending the ethological approach of studying animal behavior in the natural habitat to investigating children in their natural habitats, such as the home, school, playground, and so on (Charlesworth, 1978). Ethological research in the biological sciences emphasizes the natural environments of plants and animals as well as the related structure and evolving functions of the living organism. Moving from the domain of the fish pond to the nursery school environment, McGrew (1972) attempted to define "an ethogram for the young *Homo Sapiens*" by observing behavior patterns exhibited by 3- and 4-year-old children in social situations during nursery-school free play. Focusing on observed children's behavior patterns, such as facial expressions, gestures, postures, and locomotion, McGrew attempted to relate these observations to previous research on human and nonhuman primate behavior.

Observation of parent–child interactions including the development of attachment patterns in infancy, such as the work of Mary Ainsworth (see Ainsworth, Blehar, Waters, & Wall, 1978), has provided another focus for child development researchers. To help clarify the range of

observational methods available for studying these interpersonal relationships, Lytton (1971) proposed a hierarchy consisting of observation
of structured interaction in the laboratory, observation of unstructured
interaction in the laboratory (free play), and naturalistic observation in
the home. Components of this hierarchy reflect varying degrees of control over the situation in which observations are collected. Baumrind
(1968) has stressed that one must doubt the generalizability of observational data gathered from a rigorously controlled experimental situation to the natural family situation in which the child grows up and is
socialized.

In the tradition of ecological investigations of human behavior,
Caldwell (1969) proposed an impressive method for translating observational data into a numerical code suitable for computer analysis called
the *HOME* (*Home Observation for Measurement of the Environment*)
Inventory (see Bradley, 1982; Caldwell & Bradley, 1979). Caldwell
warned that the formulation of comprehensive theories of early childhood learning and the understanding of patterns of environmental care
will require naturalistic studies and descriptions of children functioning in different "freely constituted" environmental settings. A number
of other developmental and early childhood researchers have also recognized the problems associated with premature leaps into the laboratory, and have increasingly conducted observational studies of naturally
occurring behavior events (e.g., Charlesworth, 1978; Landesman-Dwyer,
Stein, & Sackett, 1978; White, Watts, et al., 1973).

In summary then, many child development specialists have come
to recognize that the naturalistic approach to studying human development contributes a richness, validity, and vitality not usually found
in laboratory-based research. If well-planned and carefully controlled,
such observations can yield data that are perfectly respectable from a
scientific point of view. Moreover, they often suggest hypotheses that
can undergo more intensive examination in laboratory settings. Thus,
observational approaches across the spectrum, ranging from naturalistic observation to laboratory-based observation, should be viewed as
complementary rather than as competitive routes to scientifically valid
knowledge.

OBSERVATION IN EDUCATIONAL SETTINGS

The educational context—settings, curricula, and methods—has
been the focus of observational study. Of particular interest is the role
that naturalistic observation has played in understanding the influence

of learning environments on behavior, behavioral management techniques, psychoeducational assessment, the development of criterion-referenced and curriculum-based assessment techniques, and the evaluation of curricular programs and teacher effectiveness.

Observing in Learning Environments

It is well accepted that one's genetic endowment *and* the environment in which one lives play roles *together* in affecting an individual's development. No matter how important genes might be in determining characteristics and behaviors, environments have a major impact. Children reared in an abusive family situation will generally not be as well adapted as children who grow up in a warm, supportive home. Furthermore, changes in our environment can produce changes in behavior—a phenomenon called *malleability* (Weinberg, 1983, 1989).

The influence of a child's particular learning environments has received increased attention by those seeking to understand child behavior. The multiple contexts in which the child spends time, including the home, preschool, daycare facility, religious setting, or other community environments, are all important.

Bandura (1978) proposed a *reciprocal determinism* model in which educators look at the continuous reciprocal influences of the individual child and the multiple environments in which he or she develops. The importance of this model has been well documented (e.g., Bronfenbrenner, 1977, 1979; Harms & Clifford, 1993; Hobbs, 1978; Smith & Connolly, 1980). Bronfenbrenner (1979) has detailed the important interplay of the characteristics of the environment with the characteristics and behaviors of the child. He sees the ecological environment structured like a set of nested Russian dolls in which the developing child is at the center. All of the environmental events and participants that the child perceives are important. Not only must we appreciate environmental factors, we must also look at how they influence the child, how the child experiences them, and how the child in turn affects the environment. Harms and Clifford (1993) detail the multiple external forces that influence preschool educational settings and different components of the environment surrounding and influencing the child.

The happy and friendly child and the withdrawn and cranky child will both affect their caregivers, who, in turn, will influence the children. The mutual influences of child and environment are well illustrated in the work of Werner and Smith (1992), who carried out a longitudinal study of children who were "at risk" due to environmental factors. Considerable attention has been directed to the many risk factors that impact on children, such as extreme poverty, low educational level of mothers, neglect, and unstable, unpredictable environments. However, Werner and Smith found that there are important buffers or protective factors at work in some families. Furthermore, some children in their study were more resilient than others, despite environments that placed them at risk. Important protective factors included regular time with adults who express care and interest, structure and rules in the household, consistent routines, promotion of self-esteem, a supportive relationship including a close attachment early in life, and the presence of effective reading skills by grade 4.

Some behaviors are especially influenced by the context in which they occur. How the child acquires and uses language is a prime example. Classroom observers, therefore, should focus not only on the child, but also on those environmental characteristics that are critical to fostering development. In order to understand the child's *school* behaviors, observers must also consider the characteristics and demands of the home, classroom, neighborhood, and larger communities with which the child identifies. For example, what are the demands of the home that the child experiences and the pervasive images in the community that the child sees daily? The interacting child and environmental factors that are important for the observer to review are shown in Figure 2.1.

Important characteristics of learning environments that observers need to consider (see also Unit V) include:

1. Different settings in which children spend time, including the home, neighborhood, daycare, school, and religious programs
2. Key individuals present including parents, siblings, peers, extended

FIGURE 2.1. The Child and Learning Environments

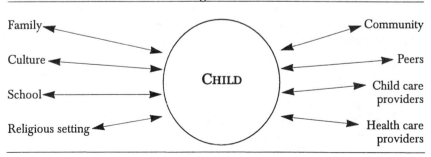

family, child care providers, teachers, religious leaders, and medical personnel
3. Materials present and their relevance to children's linguistic and cultural backgrounds and physical needs
4. Cultural expectations and language(s) spoken and language patterns modeled
5. Structure provided and consistency of routine
6. Home stressors such as divorce, substance abuse, chronic illness, and extreme poverty
7. The organization of the school environment and the demands of instruction such as
    Learning opportunities presented
    Organization of activities
    Clarity of teacher directions
    Adequacy of feedback in terms of reinforcement and the information provided
    Consistency of routines
    Language modeling and early literacy experiences
    Amount and type of practice opportunities
    Opportunities for socialization

Collecting observations from key persons in the child's life, including parents and other caregivers, and observing children engaged in their natural environments are necessary to obtain a comprehensive understanding of the environments in which the child lives.

We should be reminded that the parent is an expert about his or her child and can provide information about the child's self-help skills, motor development, language and cognitive strengths, and relationships with others. These data can be helpful in confirming or disconfirming teacher observations. Importantly, gathering observations from parents reinforces a collaborative relationship between the home and the school. Within this context, it is also important to consider the cultural and linguistic characteristics of a child's environments and how these characteristics will affect observation (Lynch & Hanson, 1992, provide useful guidelines). For example, observers should consider:

1. How they will approach cultural and language differences in what they choose to observe
2. What groups of children they will serve and how they will learn what the cultures represented by these children value and teach
3. How the cultures represented teach children to interact with adults and strangers

4. The extent to which cultural differences are at play and influence what is observed

A Mental Checklist. Observers may find it useful to develop a mental checklist to help them account for the many environmental influences, as they focus on a particular child. Consider:

Family makeup and structure
Members of the household who influence the child and the nature of these interactions
Parental expectations for the child at home and at school
Key out-of-school influences on the child (babysitter, peers, neighbors, health care providers, others)
Pervasive images the child is likely to perceive on a regular basis in the neighborhood and, if possible, at home
Home interactions/experiences that support learning and the child's concept of self
Cultural values and expectations
Parental expectations for school

One can ultimately draw a diagram of the key interacting influences of the home and the community on the child, with arrows used if desired to indicate the nature of the interaction. (Bailey, 1989, and Cantrell & Cantrell, 1985, provide details for making a systematic analysis of the environment and for considering the positive or negative nature of the interactions when planning intervention.)

Analyzing the interplay of environmental factors with child characteristics in a systematic manner can be done using a variety of approaches, with outside observers engaged in direct observation using coding systems providing the most vigorous method. While systems do not exist for all domains of early childhood behavior, good sources include Alessi and Kay (1983) and Rogers-Warren (1984).

Environmental Scales Appropriate to Early Childhood Settings. A number of scales have been developed to help understand instructional environments. A selected group will be briefly summarized here.

Ysseldyke and Christenson (1993) in *The Instructional Environment System–II (TIES-II)* focus on important components of the *classroom* for school-age children, including instructional materials, classroom management, methods and techniques for motivating learners, feedback to students, opportunities for practice, and five components of *home* environments that support learning. Information for *TIES-II* (which is a rating scale) is gained through direct observation in the classroom, teacher interview, and child interview. *TIES-II* is intended to be used to describe the learning environments of children referred for assessment and to design instructional interventions for these children, as well as to plan pre-referral interventions and to monitor changes in the quality of instruction. Ysseldyke, Christenson, and Kovaleski (1994) detail steps of a collaborative planning and intervention process in which the assessment team (including the teacher) develops and monitors alternative ways to provide relevant practice at school and at home.

The *Early Childhood Environment Rating Scale (ECERS*; Harms & Clifford, 1980) is a rating scale developed to be used in preschool settings that covers seven areas: personal care routines of children, furnishings and display for children, language-reasoning experiences, fine- and gross-motor activities, creative activities, social development, and adult needs (personal comfort and professional needs). Ratings are based on a 2–3 hour observation and interview. A classroom environment profile is yielded that can be reused to measure improvements. A modified version of the scale appropriate for use in kindergarten has been reported by Bryant, Clifford, and Peisner (1991). A number of similarly organized scales are also available to be used in child care settings including the *Infant/Toddler Environment Rating Scale* (Harms, Cryer, & Clifford, 1990), the *School-Age Care Environment Rating Scale* (Harms, Jacobs, & White, 1996), and the *Family Day Care Rating Scale* (Harms & Clifford, 1989).

The "Preschool Assessment of the Classroom Environment" (PACE; Dunst, McWilliam, & Holbert, 1986) is a rating scale that covers four broad categories of the classroom environment including program organization, environment organization, instruction, and program outcomes. Ratings are based on a 2–4 hour observation of the classroom, teacher/caregiver interview, and review of written materials. When this scale is used for purposes of intervention planning with developmentally delayed children, the teacher/caregiver also fills out the *Needs Evaluation for Educators of Developmentally Delayed Students (NEEDS*; McWilliam & Dunst, 1985), which includes the same items as the PACE stated in terms of the degree of help desired by the teacher/caretaker.

Observation in the Analysis and Management of Behavior

Influenced by the Skinnerian tradition of behaviorism and learning theory, the findings of social learning research (Baldwin, 1968; Bandura & Walters, 1963), and the pressing need for alternative ways to deal with school behavior and learning problems, preschool psychologists, special educators, and other professionals in education have developed operant conditioning and behavior management techniques appropriate for the classroom. These techniques have required education personnel to sharpen their skills in systematically observing and analyzing ongoing patterns of teacher interaction and reinforcement in the classroom and in working with caregivers in the home.

In this context, the study of reinforcing behavior in the classroom provides one example of the role of systematic observation in helping us understand the classroom learning environment. Teachers' use of verbal approval and disapproval has been consistently observed to be effective in decreasing inappropriate pupil behaviors and in increasing desired pupil behaviors (O'Leary & O'Leary, 1972). The content of these approvals and disapprovals and the characteristics of the pupils to whom they are directed are important in understanding classroom life. One interesting procedure, the *Teacher Approval and Disapproval Observation Record* (*TAD*), developed by White, Beecher, and colleagues (1973) and White (1975), allows the observer to record teacher verbal approval and disapproval patterns as well as pupil variables and the preceding pupil behaviors to which the teacher had reacted.

Using the *TAD*, Waters (1973) studied gender differences in verbal approval and disapproval rates among teachers in first, second, and third grades. She found that there were no differences in the rates of approval given to boys and girls, but that boys received significantly more disapproval. Beecher (1973), studying teacher verbal approval and disapproval patterns in prekindergarten, kindergarten, and first-grade classrooms, observed different approval patterns at each grade level, but similar disapproval patterns across these grades. Observation studies such as these are of importance in understanding the existing reinforcement practices of teachers, given the potency of reinforcement in the classroom.

Observation is also key to behavioral assessment techniques used at the early childhood levels to help teachers and parents deal more effectively with such behaviors as temper tantrums, fighting, and hyperactivity. Behavioral assessment is integrally linked with intervention. During behavioral assessment, observation involves a number of steps including collecting baseline data prior to intervention, keeping track of changes during intervention, and maintaining a record of a child's behavior after an intervention ceases in order to determine the effectiveness of the intervention and to determine if the desired behavior is maintained. Barnett and Carey (1992), in *Designing Interventions for Preschool Learning and Behavior Problems*, provide many examples of the use of behavioral observation in the design of interventions.

For readers interested in pursuing this topic further, the Bibliography of this book includes selected references for implementing behavior management techniques.

Observation and Psychoeducational Assessment

Pupil learning and behavior are areas of particular concern to most early childhood educators. In their daily interactions with pupils, teachers are continually assessing the degree to which desired learning goals are being reached. Indeed, observation is an integral, key component of case study and teacher self-assessment. Almy and Genishi (1981), in *Ways of Studying Children;* Genishi (1992), in *Ways of Assessing Children and Curriculum;* Cohen, Stern, and Balaban (1996), in *Observing and Recording the Behavior of Young Children;* and Nicolson and Shipstead (1994), in *Through the Looking Glass: Observations in the Early Childhood Classroom,* have all detailed how observation can be used as an integral component in assessing young children in school settings. Observation consistently is viewed as the major tool for assessing the learning needs of young children because it focuses on children engaged in naturally occurring everyday tasks, in contrast to the often unfamiliar tasks presented in formal testing situations (Bagnato & Neisworth, 1992; Barnett & Carey, 1992; Boehm & Brassard, in press). In addition, it is the only way to explore many child behaviors such as the nature of peer interactions, attention span, and emotional characteristics.

In "Guidelines for Appropriate Curriculum Content and Assessment in Programs Serving Children Ages 3 Through 8" (1991), the National Association for the Education of Young Children (NAEYC) and the National Association of Early Childhood Specialists in State Departments of Education (NAECS/SDE) set forth eight key principles of developmentally appropriate practice. Principles such as these can be followed by teachers in their classrooms, by both home- and center-based child care providers, and by specialists. Clearly, observational assessment is central to providing developmentally appropriate curriculum and intervention and to tracking developmental changes over time. Observation is essential to identifying the development of skills across behavioral domains, understanding the approaches and strategies children use to solve problems, and being aware of the supports and activities teachers and parents use to encourage children's best performance. Combined with work samples, observation is central to curriculum-based assessment (assessment directly linked to the goals and activities of classroom instruction) and other alternative assessment approaches, such as portfolio assessment (the systematic ongoing collection and review of children's work samples), widely viewed as appropriate for young children.

Teachers are the primary assessors as children engage in typical everyday activities, and they are able to use their findings to provide appropriate instruction. Except in the case of children who have special learning needs, standardized tests for school entry or readiness decisions based on kindergarten achievement are being viewed with increasing skepticism. Widely adhered to position statements (NAEYC, NAECS/SDE, 1991) advise that a test *should not* be used to determine school entry or readiness, and a test *should not* be the sole criterion for retention in kindergarten or placement in special programs. The goal is for assessment to be relevant to curricular goals and content and to provide teachers with information useful for planning their instructional activities and for monitoring the effects of intervention. Observation is essential to current best practices for ecologically based assessment (Shapiro & Skinner, 1990).

When diagnostic assessment is indicated and formal tests are used, assessors increasingly appreciate the importance of collecting observations from key people in the child's life, describing the influence of various settings and situations on the child's behavior, and determining the demands of learning environments in order to understand what is needed for children to perform successfully and changes that might facilitate their development. Collecting observations from key people in the child's life provides *converging* or *disconfirming* information from different perspectives. Gathering observations of a child within various natural contexts (home, school, playground) can generate rich developmental information regarding the child's current methods for coping with day-to-day situations, as well as his or her problem-solving strategies for particular tasks (Keogh, 1972). In collaboration with the classroom teacher, the school social worker, and parents, the school psychologist and special educator can observe the child's interactions with peers in the classroom and other settings, and, on another level, can view the ways in which the child relates to adults. Implicit in this process is the comparison of each child's performance with behavioral norms concerning children of a similar age and background developed by the observer over time and as provided through sources such as developmental checklists, normative data, and developmental research.

Observations within the formal testing situation are important sources of information not only to support or question the confidence the school psychologist, learning disabilities specialist, and teacher place in their findings, but also to raise additional questions about children's behavior. These individuals can observe the gestures, actions, and other nonverbal behaviors that often contribute meaningful assessment data to written test protocols (see Alessi & Kay, 1983; Baker & Tyne, 1980). Behavioral evidence is provided regarding the child's ease in relating to the tasks presented during assessment, rapport with the examiner, and general interest in the tasks. During individual testing and observational assessment, behavioral information gained through purposeful observation might also include:

- Time taken to complete tasks.
- Approach to tasks—e.g., does child attempt difficult tasks or give up?
- Speed and accuracy of response—i.e., does child respond:
    Immediately and accurately?
    Immediately and then change answers?
    Immediately and does not consider alternatives?
    Slowly, but accurately?
- Amount of encouragement required—e.g., does child keep asking if he or she is doing well?
- Activity level of the child—i.e., does the child:
    Stay in seat with little movement?
    Stay in seat with repeated shifting around?
    Get out of seat occasionally?
    Get out of seat repeatedly?
- Amount of spontaneous talking the child does and the samples of language yielded through these exchanges.
- Physical features of the child (such as whether or not child wears glasses).
- Attention span?
- Ability to follow questions?

During group testing, the observer can record such things as:

- Time taken by various children to complete tasks.
- Children who have difficulty with presented instructions or in keeping their place.
- Which children skip difficult items, spend all their time on a few items, seem to be marking answers randomly, or repeatedly look around the room.

The skill of the assessor in making, recording, and integrating these observations with other sources of data is key. Generally, observations made during assessment are not carried out in a systematic way. A number of researchers (Glutting, McDermott, & Oakland, 1989; Kaplan, 1993) have conducted studies to determine the usefulness of observations carried out during testing. Their studies document that assessors are sensitive to behaviors that affect children's performance on intelligence tests, but that these observations do not generalize to children's behavior in situations outside the testing situation, such as academic performance in the classroom. Thus, test-related observations should be considered hunches to be followed up by observation in the child's natural environment.

Interest in studying children's problem-solving strategies and intellectual styles has encouraged the observation of behavior in classrooms and test situations that reflect these strategies and styles (Bruner, Goodnow, & Austin, 1956; Ginsburg, 1987; Kagan & Kogan, 1970; Keogh, 1972; Kogan, 1983). These observations can help the assessor in matching psychoeducational interventions to the particular educational needs of a child.

Observation techniques are particularly useful for understanding the learning needs and environments of young children with special educational requirements. For example, observing the behavior of a hearing-impaired child or a physically disabled pupil who has been placed in a "mainstream" classroom can provide ongoing data regarding the child's adjustment, the extent to which the classroom environment has been modified to accommodate the child's needs, and the appropriateness of the educational placement. Several investigators highlight the use of observation strategies to improve the educational experiences of exceptional children (Cantrell & Cantrell, 1985; Dunst, McWilliam, & Holbert, 1986; Gitler & Gordon, 1979; Greenwood & Carta, 1987; Kaufman, Agard, & Semmel, 1985; Rogers-Warren, 1984; and Semmel, 1975, are just a few examples).

Also, the assessment of adaptive behavior among institutionalized and noninstitutionalized mentally retarded, emotionally maladjusted, and developmentally disabled children has been dependent on the use of reliable rating scales and behavioral checklists such as *AAMD (American Association on Mental Deficiency) Adaptive Behavior Scale—School Edition* (Lambert, Windmiller, Cole, & Tharinger, 1981); the *Vineland Adaptive Behavior Scales* (Sparrow, Balla, & Cichetti, 1984); and the *Preschool Behavior Questionnaire* (see Sattler, 1988).

Determining the optimal teaching techniques or interventions for children with learning problems—in reading, for instance—can often be accomplished efficiently by informal diagnostic procedures that include direct observation of children's oral and silent reading behavior. The observant classroom teacher can recognize children who display symptoms suggestive of reading disability, engage in systematic observation, and try a variety of intervention strategies. These data can then be used as a basis for referral to other professionals for intervention programming.

When working with children who present special needs, assessors are likely to continue to use tests and other appropriate strategies including the techniques of objective observation to raise and then confirm or reject hypotheses about an individual's functioning and the contribution of environmental factors, and to develop appropriate intervention strategies. Those engaged in psychoeducational assessment should seek naturalistic behavioral data to support their inferences. In fact, Public Law 94-142, the Education for All Handicapped Children Act of 1975 (and its downward extension, PL 99-457, now amended by PL 101-476, the Individuals with Disabilities Education Act—IDEA), has mandated the use of systematic, naturalistic observation techniques as complements to standardized testing practices (Heller, Holtzman, & Messick, 1982). Furthermore, in determining the effectiveness of various intervention or remediation approaches, the school professional, needing to base conclusions on observable changes in behavior, has increasingly drawn on naturalistic observation data to document the impact of the intervention program.

Throughout the assessment process, teachers play a key role. In order to evaluate their unique impact in early childhood classrooms and with individual children, teachers need to reflect on their own practices (see Hills, 1993; Schweinhart, 1993; Shepard, 1994). An Early Childhood Teacher/Observer Self Check is presented in Figure 2.2 to help teachers engage in this process.

Observation and Assessment Related to the Curriculum

The use of systematic observation techniques is particularly crucial in facilitating a "match" between a child's current level of functioning and the educational experiences to which he or she is exposed (see, for example, Bagnato & Neisworth, 1992; Bloom, Hastings, & Madaus, 1971; Shapiro, 1987). Observations are important in formulating goals, selecting appropriate teaching procedures for working with individual children, monitoring progress, and evaluating the effectiveness of instruction or of a particular behavioral intervention. To provide a curricular match for the individual pupil, the classroom teacher must routinely assess whether a particular learning skill is being demonstrated and at what level (Boehm, 1973). Increasingly, observation-

FIGURE 2.2. **An Early Childhood Teacher/Observer Self Check**

Check yourself on the following characteristics with relation to your instructional environment:

1. Do I have beliefs about what is appropriate behavior for young children based on their chronological age? What are these beliefs, and how are they likely to influence my teaching or intervention practices?

2. Am I knowledgeable about the cultural characteristics of the children I serve and how their cultural experiences are likely to affect the observations I make?

3. How do I interact with and view children/families who are linguistically different from me?

4. Have I observed the child's comprehension of task directions and provided further prompts or other assistance?

5. How does the child respond to help, such as breaking down tasks into smaller units?

6. How does the child respond to my encouragement of efforts or other reinforcement techniques that I use? Are my reinforcements appropriate? Does the child demonstrate confidence in self?

7. What have I done to make tasks motivating to the child? Have these attempts been effective?

8. Have I investigated the child's learning strategies and problem-solving approaches?

9. Have I explored environmental constraints and facilitating factors in the home? In the school and/or daycare setting? For example, are there regular, consistent routines? Is there a caring adult who spends times regularly with the child? What is the nature of the child's language interactions? What kinds of early literacy experiences are presented?

10. What kinds of learning opportunities do I offer, and how are these matched to the needs of the child?

based alternative assessment procedures are being advocated to replace standardized testing in early childhood classrooms. Alternative assessment procedures include criterion-referenced assessment, curriculum-based assessment (CBA), and play assessment. The teacher is key to collecting and organizing observational information along with work samples that document skill acquisition across major developmental domains. A brief description of these approaches follows.

Criterion-referenced testing is one form of assessment specifically related to the problem of the match. The question posed by this form of assessment is "To what extent is each pupil proficient in attaining the goal or goals of an instructional unit?" The criterion-referenced test, by definition, must be related to the objectives of an instructional unit. In turn, these instructional objectives must be stated in behavioral terms and broken down into their component parts. An additional consideration may be the variety of contexts in which assessment focuses on what the individual child can or cannot do relative to a given objective. Systematic observation is integral to the development and use of criterion-referenced tests. For example, if an educational objective is to evaluate self-help skills as they develop in young children, it would be necessary to define what is meant by self-help skills, consider which self-help skills would be of concern and when and in what contexts they might be demonstrated, and evaluate the individual child's progress by creating and using an observation procedure.

The criterion-referenced test may be contrasted with the more widely used norm-referenced test, which addresses itself to the issues of differentiating pupil achievement and making predictions. Although both forms of assessment are useful in educational settings, the distinction in purpose is critical. With *norm-referenced* tests the score of one child is compared with the scores of others, but with criterion-referenced measures children are compared with themselves as they move toward mastery. Some useful resources in this area include Gagné (1985), Glaser and Nitko (1971), Gronlund (1985), Martuza (1977), and Popham (1971).

Curriculum-based assessment has diverse forms (see, for example, Shinn, Rosenfield, & Knutson, 1989), which share many of the same features as criterion-referenced assessment. Curriculum-based assessment is based on observing the child's progress in relationship to curricula used by the school. At the preschool level, CBA can sample commonly emphasized goals or a particular curriculum. Again, this form of assessment provides information that helps teachers set learning objectives and track the mastery of skills, particularly within developmentally sequenced curricula (Neisworth & Bagnato, 1988). One advantage of this form of assessment is a direct match between the curricula and assessment and assessment's direct link to intervention (Bagnato & Neisworth, 1992; Shapiro, 1987). The information yielded from CBA is immediately useful for teachers in helping them to evaluate the extent to which children have mastered instructional goals, to modify instruction, and to set new goals.

However, neither criterion-referenced nor curriculum-based assessment procedures address other factors relating to mastery, such as the strategies children use to solve problems, the kinds of adult assistance needed to help children move toward mastery, the effects of feedback and reinforcement, the time allocated to instruction, and so forth (see, for example, Lentz & Shapiro, 1986; Shapiro, 1987).

The importance of *play* in the early childhood curriculum is well recognized. Research has focused on play as an integral part of cognitive development reflecting children's ways of thinking and problem solving (Piaget, 1962) and as a means through which children stretch their abilities (Vygotsky, 1978). A central premise of Vygotsky's theory is that if a child cannot do something alone, he or she may be successful with the assistance of a more cognitively aware person who facilitates development through modeling and assistance. This concept also serves as the basis for what is referred to as "dynamic assessment" with a young child (see, for example, Lidz, 1991). A strong research literature supports play as influencing cognitive development, social-emotional development, language usage, and physical and motor development. It is understandable, therefore, why play increasingly is seen as an avenue for assessment, particularly with children who do not speak English and children with handicapping conditions. Observation of children's play behaviors can be used for identifying teaching/intervention goals and tracking a child's progress in relationship to these goals. While there are many different formats for play assessment, ranging from free-play observation to highly structured play situations (Schaefer, Gitlin, & Sandgrund, 1991), Linder (1993a) has developed a comprehensive approach to the assessment of play referred to as *Transdisciplinary Play-Based Assessment (TPBA)*. TPBA is implemented by a team including parents and experts in different developmental domains who observe a child engaged during different phases of play activity with a play facilitator. Guidelines for the observation of cognitive, socioemotional, communication and language, and motor development are used to assist team members in determining what skills and limitations the child has. Using toys the child finds appealing, *TPBA* represents natural tasks and serves as the avenue for intervention. The information gathered through observation is used to form a program plan for the child (also see Linder, 1993b, "Transdisciplinary Play-Based Intervention"). Another procedure using play as an avenue to review development and generate an intervention plan for children with disabilities is detailed in *Using the Supportive Play Model: Individualized Intervention in Early Childhood Practice* (Sheridan, Foley, & Radlinski, 1995).

A thorough exploration of the issues related to the pros and cons of alternative assessment strategies is beyond the scope of this book. The point to be made here is that direct observation is key to the alternative assessment approaches.

Observing the Effectiveness of Curriculum and Teaching Practices

Within classrooms, systematic observation has been used to generate information regarding the nature and effectiveness of varying instructional strategies (e.g., Good & Brophy, 1991). This book is not intended to present an in-depth exploration of these strategies, but some areas of application of systematic observation in studying the effectiveness of classroom practices may be of interest to the reader.

Flanders (1975) provided a framework for analyzing classroom interactions by observing teacher and pupil verbal behavior. Interaction-analysis activities have provided the basis for pre- and in-service education programs that help teachers develop and control their specific teaching behaviors. The popularity of the Flanders Interaction Analysis Model has been reflected in a burgeoning research literature in teacher effectiveness that has focused on discovering relationships between teacher behavior and measures of pupil growth (Good & Brophy, 1991; Joyce & Weil, 1972; Stallings, 1977). Also, Good and Brophy (1991) present numerous formats related to collecting observational data in areas such as

- Managing behavior in the classroom
- The use of motivational strategies
- Mastery learning
- Small-group work and cooperative learning opportunities
- Instructional activities including questioning and scaffolding student work; fostering higher-order thinking and problem-solving strategies; presenting information to students; feedback; and structuring activities and assignments

In addition, they have presented the *Brophy-Good Dyadic Interaction System* (Good & Brophy, 1970) which is used to document the extent to which individual students receive more or less of certain teacher actions than others, such as questions asked and the nature of feedback.

With this understanding of the vital role that observational methods can play in the study of children, the educational process, and learning settings, let us begin to unravel the complexities of the observation process and to develop the skills necessary for systematic observation in early-learning settings.

The Forms of Observation

There is a wide range of written forms that our observations in learning environments can take, from informal, qualitative descriptions to quantitative recording formats. These forms of observation include *narrative* approaches in which observers write down what they see and hear (diary descriptions, anecdotes, and specimen records), *judgment-based approaches* (checklists and ratings scales), and *formal observation schedules*. We will briefly describe these alternative modes of observing, highlighting their uses and limitations. Each of these forms of observation is going to be influenced by the user's prior knowledge of the child and/or family, personal biases or preconceived beliefs, experiences, and understanding of the developmental literature. These user differences will be reflected in the situations one chooses to observe, the level of precision one uses, and the outcomes one cites.

NARRATIVE FORMS

Diary Descriptions

Maintaining diary accounts of changes in human growth, behavior, and developmental events or milestones is the oldest observational method (Wright, 1960, 1967). Diary descriptions of young children's development have been kept by relatives, caretakers, and other observers close to the children. Diary entries are recorded in a narrative style and may vary from brief daily entries to comprehensive detailed accounts. The careful documentation of children's development in natural contexts can provide a strong data base for formulating hypotheses about human development, which in turn can be investigated through other methods of inquiry (laboratory experiments, field studies, and so forth).

The lack of reliability and the unsystematic nature of these descriptions are potential problems. Another drawback is that diary accounts are almost always limited to one subject or, at best, a few subjects, making interpretations and generalizations difficult. Nevertheless, regular diary descriptions do provide a record of the continuity of behavior over time and can help one to identify meaningful patterns in development. Numerous independent diary descriptions of, for example, children's language acquisition have led to an increased objective understanding of typical developmental and universal norms. These accounts may be accompanied by photographs, video, and samples of a child's productions to document the child's unfolding behaviors.

Anecdotal Records, Field Notes, Logs

Observers can write brief descriptive summaries or notes of their observations in any situation. These can range from developmental milestones—"Mario took his first step today"—to behavioral events— "Mary was enthusiastic about her work when writing about our class outing"—to important incidents such as a fist fight or a seizure. Although anecdotes can be important objective descriptions of events, they can also be subjective statements about these events. Many of us recall "comments" sections on school records, which often included anecdotal observations such as "has difficulty relating" or "a pleasure to have in class." These comments were passed on from one teacher to the next. In the past, unfavorable records could follow a child throughout his or her school career, perhaps biasing a new teacher's views of the pupil. Currently, many states prohibit the inclusion of such anecdotal accounts in official school records. However, teachers use anecdotes frequently. Many early childhood classrooms today, for example, use holistic instructional approaches in literacy that require teachers to document the emergence of each child's behaviors in areas of instructional concern such as reading and writing. Systematic collection of these teacher notes is important when teachers maintain portfolios to document children's development and the skills they have mastered.

When they are factual accounts, anecdotal records, field notes, and logs can provide rich descriptive information related to child development. Anecdotal records can be made by teachers, child care workers, parents, physicians, or other specialists at regular intervals (but many times at irregular intervals) to maintain a "factual" record. Anecdotes may or may not include what led up to or followed a recorded incident such as a temper tantrum. The choice of events to be recorded, timeliness of the record, and amount of detail provided are determined by the observer, who can choose to document unusual or unexpected events. Anecdotal records often reflect the biases of the observer or the lack of familiarity with cultural and linguistic differences. A number of procedures have been suggested for preparing and interpreting anecdotal records (see, e.g., Cartwright & Cartwright, 1984; Irwin & Bushnell, 1980; Thorndike & Hagen, 1977). These include techniques such as:

- Limiting discussion to one incident
- Recording events as soon as possible after they occur, including the date and specific details and sequence of the events
- Separating interpretive comments from factual reporting; setting up the recording sheet to facilitate this distinction
- Considering supportive evidence (such as photographs of children's work products)
- Providing information about the context in which the observations took place

Clearly, although anecdotes and field notes can provide an understanding of behaviors not easily appraised by other means—such as social skills, adjustments, and health status—along with instructionally relevant responses to teaching activities, it is critical that objective, factual reporting take place and that follow-up study be made of behaviors of concern. Consideration must also be given to how typical or representative noted behaviors are for the individual child and for his or her peers. Out of context, anecdotes may assume undue importance; within context, they can provide important insights into children's behavior and successful or less successful teaching strategies, as well as enrich discussions with other professionals and parents.

Maintaining regular logs for individual children can be very useful. These can be used as a source for developing other observational forms. They can also be useful in understanding the development of children's skills and behaviors. However, keeping track of the hundreds of observations a teacher makes every day is very challenging. Some suggestions that teachers and child care workers have made include using different colored index cards for different areas of development (referred to as "notable moment" cards by Wright & Borland, 1993) and using brief key words when taking notes, which can later be transcribed into meaningful sentences (Nicolson & Shipstead, 1994). Time must be set aside for organizing the anecdotes or field notes collected for each child into developmental areas. One suggested format is shown in Figure 3.1.

Specimen Records

Specimen records are closely related to diary descriptions but represent the "continuous observing and narrative recording of a behavior

FIGURE 3.1. Sample Format for Organizing Anecdotal Information

Child: _____   Observer: _____

Developmental Domain	Date	Environmental Context	Observation	Inference/Comments

sequence under chosen conditions of time and life setting" (Wright, 1960, p. 83). Observers detail the setting and record everything they see or hear. Thus, behavior is described in its natural context. The resulting record is then reviewed and analyzed. Specimen records are useful to note small changes in development or behavior that occur over time. A classic example is provided in *One Boy's Day* (Barker & Wright, 1951), a record of "what a seven-year-old boy did and what his home and school and neighborhood and town did to him from the time he awoke one morning until he went to sleep that night" (p. 1). Eight observers, all adults familiar to the child, took turns during the day recording all directly observable behaviors, including vocalizations and body movements. They also recorded their own impressions. The extensive information gathered was later analyzed and a categorization of behaviors and identification of behavior sequences made.

Specimen records provide comprehensive accounts of behavior and are useful for establishing the range and types of behaviors a person may exhibit in a given situation. They may serve as a basis for formulating observational questions and developing structured observation procedures, and can be used for detailed analyses and quantitative study. Although extremely valuable, specimen records are especially time consuming and costly. The use of audiotapes and particularly videotapes can enhance the reliability and completeness of this form of observation. Accompanying information must be included to clarify the nature of the setting and activities in which children are engaged.

Within the classroom, the teacher can engage in a brief form of specimen-record observation, generally referred to as a *running record*.

For example, the teacher may choose to maintain a running record of everything a child does and says during an activity such as conversation, drawing, writing, peer interaction, and so forth. The example that follows involves a child engaged in an assigned reading activity. Five minutes of such recording may result in important insights.

A SAMPLE RUNNING RECORD

Subject: Tom
Setting: Second-grade classroom, 31 students
Situation: Class members were to work independently on a reading assignment that included a reading passage with five questions written on the chalkboard.
Observation time: 10 minutes
Observer: Judith Zucker

Tom held a looseleaf in his lap. His reader was opened to the appropriate page on his desk. His desk was cluttered with other books and pencils.

T. wrote for approximately 2 minutes. He copied questions from the board, seemingly looking at the board after writing each word of a particular question. He completed the copying of only one question by the end of the 2-minute span.

T. stopped writing and began to play with the tape dispenser that was in his desk. He tore off pieces of tape and pasted them on the inside of his desk. During this time he spoke to himself using the phrases: "Oh boy," when he tore off an exceptionally long piece of tape; "Just one more piece," after which he did stop tearing; "What's the next question?," looking at the board but not copying; and "Ick!" During the time T. looked at the board, he held a small piece of tape between his thumb and forefinger and moved his forefinger toward and away from the tape.

He began to write again. (I reminded the class to answer questions in complete sentences.) T. grimaced. He began to search inside his desk for a pencil. He found one, examined it, rejected it, found another pencil with an eraser. T. spent roughly 2 minutes erasing all of what was written on his paper thus far. He brushed away the eraser remains. He stated, not too quietly, "Uh oh! My paper ripped."

T. attempted to repair the paper with tape. He tore off a piece of tape. He made an unhappy face—apparently the piece of tape was too small. He started to tear off a second piece but lost the end of the roll of tape. He put his hand to his head. He tried to find

> the end of the tape again. He struggled with the tape for almost a minute, scraping the roll with his fingernail.
>
> Defeated, he tore a sheet of paper out of the looseleaf and elaborately crumpled it. He placed the looseleaf on his desk slowly, put his head down, placed two hands on the desk, and pushed himself away from the desk. He stood, extending his arms to both sides, stretched, looked at me and walked slowly to the wastebasket carrying the paper. He threw the paper in the basket, walked to my desk, and said, "Miss Z., my paper is ripped."
>
> T. returned to his seat. He began to look for a pencil and clean paper. He repositioned the looseleaf and reader as before. He began to write his name on the paper.

Running records are helpful for teachers and care providers to detail child behaviors across all developmental areas—speech and language, perceptual, cognitive, motor, social, and emotional behavior, as well as self-help skills. These records are a good source of data about the range of children's behavior displayed in natural contexts. They also provide us with a minute-by-minute account of ongoing behavior and help us understand where a child is developmentally, the strategies a child uses to deal with everyday tasks, and the influences of the actions of the teacher and other children.

Running records can also be used as the basis for formulating more specific observational questions or for individualizing instruction to meet a child's needs. They allow observers to witness the full range of behaviors displayed in a given situation and review these observations at a later point in time. Thus, running records allow observers to gain insight not only into *what* behaviors occurred, but also into the *context* in which they were made and the sequence of behaviors including their *antecedents* and their *consequences*. This approach allows the observer to focus his or her attention on one individual and provides an opportunity to become acutely aware of behaviors of the child that may have previously gone undetected. Running records can be used to help us understand children's behavior: oral language, following directions, attention span, fine-motor control, task completion, interpersonal interactions, and emergent literacy.

Collecting running records over time will help teachers arrive at inferences backed by specific behavioral information. Teale (1990), for example, points out how important a teacher's observations are in tracking emergent literacy. During group storybook reading, the teacher can focus on one or two children per day, noting such variables as attention to tasks, recall of key facts, comprehension of stories, and participation. Running records also are useful as a preliminary step to developing checklists, rating scales, and systematic observation systems, described below.

Limitations to running records include (1) the requirement of intense concentration and, therefore, the difficulty of carrying out these observations over long periods of time and (2) the impossibility of recording all of a subject's behaviors, due to the recorder's inability to write fast enough. The use of audiotape or videotape, although solving these problems, introduces others (see Unit X). However, by taping sessions and transcribing them, observers can track developmental patterns over time such as the use of words or sentences, along with gestures to convey needs and decide on the next instructional or intervention steps.

To facilitate the collection of running records:

- Set up a format that helps you keep track of your observations in sequence. If, for example, you are interested in how long a child has persisted with a task, include minute-by-minute recording.
- Keep track of exactly what happens, including what the child says and does, as well as the situation. Use objective, precise, descriptive vocabulary so that you or another reader can understand exactly what happened (including details and the order of events).
- Provide descriptors of the context including who was present, to whom a child's actions were directed, the materials present or used, and what was taking place.
- Note times when activities changed and how they changed.
- Try to analyze the record soon after it is completed. For example, underline and count key behaviors, instructional acts, or other contextual events.

A general format is suggested in Figure 3.2.

JUDGMENT-BASED APPROACHES

In contrast to diary descriptions, anecdotes, and specimen records, checklists and rating scales require a judgment on the part of the observer.

Checklists

Checklists involve a listing of behaviors that, generally, are marked as being present or absent; other behaviors are ignored. Therefore, they

FIGURE 3.2. **Running Record Format**

Child_____   Time_____

Date_____   Activity_____

Observer_____

Description of context:

Running record observations in sequence:

Time   Comments

_____

_____

_____

_____

etc.

Interpretations/hunches:

are a dichotomous form of rating that involve a summary judgment on the part of the observer. Only infrequently, however, is detailed descriptive information provided about the *quality* of behavior. Increasingly, checklists are being used by teachers to track the development of behaviors of interest across settings and over time. (Checklists usually are *sign systems*, a topic discussed in Unit VI.) Checklists are easy to complete and, therefore, are widely used in early childhood assessment. Checklists are available commercially or teachers can create their own. They may be completed while actually observing the child, but are more frequently completed "after the fact" from memory. One advantage of checklists is that they can be completed by several individuals, all of whom focus on the same child and therefore provide convergent or divergent information (an important check on validity).

Checklists can help child care workers, parents, and teachers understand a variety of behaviors such as self-help, expressive language, and fine-motor skills. In order to develop a useful checklist, behaviors must be clearly defined and listed beforehand—the usefulness of the checklist depends on whether it includes all possible key behaviors (Fewell, 1984). In order to generate this list, one must carry out a *task analysis* that requires the developer to ask, for example, "What does the child need to be able to do to demonstrate self-help skills in dressing?" "Under what conditions, specifically, might these behaviors be demonstrated?" "What kinds of adult supports does the child need to be successful?" Many areas of complex behavior, such as peer relationships or task-appropriate behavior, can be analyzed (broken down into their component parts and organized hierarchically) through this approach. Thus, checklists can reflect a teacher's curriculum and/or behavioral objectives and can help focus observers. Furthermore, several checklists can be used concurrently.

A number of checklists are presented next as a guide to readers. Such checklists are especially integral to developmental and performance-based assessment.

- The "Child Skills Checklist" (Beaty, 1993) is designed for use by teachers in regular classrooms. The "Child Skills Checklist" covers the areas of self-identity; emotional development; social play; prosocial behavior; large-motor development; small-motor development; cognitive development: classification and seriation; cognitive development: number, time, space, memory; spoken language; written language; art skills; and imagination. Typical classroom behaviors are listed under each category and teachers check each item they see the child perform regularly, along with the date and supportive evidence (citing specific examples). Teaching activities are detailed for each developmental area by Beaty so that there is a clear link between checklist and instruction.
- The *Hawaii Early Learning Profile* (HELP; Furuno et al., 1979) provides a graphic display of the progression of a child's abilities in six domains: cognitive, language, gross-motor, fine-motor, social, and self-help. This checklist spans from birth through 3 years of age and is a comprehensive assessment tool integrating information into an intervention program.
- The *Work Sampling System* (Jablon, Marsden, & Meisels, 1993) consists of three complementary components: (1) developmental check-

lists and guidelines, (2) portfolios of children's work, and (3) summary reports completed by teachers. This system is available for children from 3 years of age through fifth grade and contains detailed descriptions of child learning behaviors that can contribute to learning objectives.

(See also *Watching Children Read and Write: Observational Records for Children with Special Needs* [Kemp, 1987], which helps teachers focus on specific items related to the processes of reading and writing.)

Unfortunately, not all checklists are well detailed or task analyzed. Many are superficial and cover only small samples of behavior, demanding that the user review the content of a potential checklist carefully to consider the adequacy of the information yielded. Other problems relate to such issues as bias and selectivity. Checklists can reflect a particular theoretical or cultural perspective and can provide a biased view of the observational situation. Finally, checklists usually do not provide information regarding the degree or frequency with which a behavior is exhibited. Checklists that provide space for narrative elaboration can help users evaluate the extent or degree to which the observed behaviors are exhibited.

Within classroom settings, depending on the user's purpose, checklists can be developed and maintained for each child or for the class as a whole. A general format is provided in Figure 3.3 as a guide for teachers developing their own checklists. When developing one's own checklist, many of the same procedures should be followed as are detailed later for developing observation systems.

In a nutshell, when considering the use of checklists, observers must engage in the following steps:

1. Review the checklist and determine if the items are clear and cover the content area of interest in sufficient detail to track a child's progress and to establish meaningful teaching goals or behavioral interventions.

FIGURE 3.3. **Checklist General Format**

Behaviors	**Date**	**Context**	**Comments**
List specific behaviors	Date(s) observed	Specify the situation	Ideas, notes about the intensity of the behavior, etc.

2. Practice using the checklist, with a co-observer if possible, to determine the ease with which judgments can be made and the extent to which another observer is likely to note the same behaviors. Discuss with the co-observer agreements and disagreements and refine the behaviors specified.
3. Consider the special needs presented by children, such as the hearing-impaired, or behaviors likely to be demonstrated by children from different cultural groups and determine whether these are reflected in the procedures used.
4. Consider important related behaviors and issues not covered in the checklist that relate to child functioning, such as teacher interactions, the appropriateness of materials, and issues related to the setting.
5. Consider supportive evidence supplied with the checklist, such as data related to its technical adequacy and related studies.

Rating Scales

Rating scales focus on designated behaviors and allow observers to judge the extent or degree to which these behaviors are exhibited. Most published rating scales require judgment based on overall impressions and are often used in the assessment of personality and social adjustment or physical motor development. Although ratings can be made while observing ongoing behaviors, they frequently are made on the basis of past observations and are completed when the child is not present. Rating scales utilize numbers or descriptive phrases (see Figure 3.4).

One example of a recent rating scale is the *High/Scope Child Observation Record* (*COR*; High/Scope Educational Research Foundation, 1992). *COR* was developed to be used across preschool programs, particularly those that use the High/Scope Curriculum (Hohmann, Banet, & Weikart, 1979) to assess the developmental status of young children. *COR* is based on brief observational notes of teachers describing young children's behavior in six developmental domains. These notes are then used as the basis for classifying children's behavior on an item rating scale.

Although ratings tell us nothing about the causes of behaviors, they can help us to describe or pinpoint specific behaviors. The observer must make a summary judgment about the most descriptive behavior or provide a numerical rating. Bias and lack of sufficient opportunity to observe can influence judgment, particularly when numerical scores or broad descriptors are solely used or where the target behaviors are not directly

FIGURE 3.4. **Forms of Rating Scales**

A. Numbers used to rank behaviors of interest from high to low, such as:

Easily relates to classmates			Has difficulty relating to classmates	
1	2	3	4	5

B. Descriptive phrases of attitudes, such as:

Is attentive to teacher directions

Very Attentive	Generally Attentive	Often Inattentive	Very Inattentive

C. Specific qualities or objectives stated in terms of performance, such as:

Unable to print name	Prints first name only	Prints first & last initial	Prints first & last name

observable and therefore require inferences to be drawn by the observer. Consider the challenges, for example, when observers make the judgments required in Figure 3.4B. Caution also must be exercised with scales that provide midpoint scores such as in Figure 3.4A. When using these kinds of scales there is a tendency for observers to rate at the midpoint and to avoid extreme judgments (errors of central tendency).

Kerlinger (1973) has suggested that rating scales are particularly susceptible to a number of sources of bias, including the "halo effect" (positive judgments based on past experience or knowledge), error of severity, error of leniency, and error of central tendency (see Unit VII). Kerlinger has also pointed out that the "halo effect is extremely difficult to avoid. It seems to be particularly strong in traits that are not clearly defined, not easily observable, and that are morally important" (p. 549). When behaviors are emerging, observers often want to give the child the benefit of the doubt. This tendency is more problematic when rating scales are used during assessment rather than as a part of ongoing classroom life.

Rating scales, however, have the advantage of being easy to use and applicable to a wide variety of situations. They can help focus an observer's attention, particularly when points along the scale are behaviorally defined: The more observable and precise each point, the greater the objectivity of the results. It is important as well to be aware of the limitations of rating scales. In particular, they do not indicate the *reasons* for a child's performance, and they do not suggest the *form* of the next teaching or intervention activities. The advantages of rating scales and their ease of use lead to three cautions. First, it is essential that ratings be based on a sufficient number of observations across activities to arrive at a valid (rather than superficial) judgment. Second, observers must be mindful that many rating scales do not specify precise behaviors and should be aware of their own sensitivities, knowledge of cultural variations, and biases in making ratings. A third challenge for the rater is knowledge of typical developmental sequences and normal ranges of child variability.

The steps detailed for considering the use of checklists apply as well to rating scales. When considering the use of published rating scales, it is important to review the manuals for supportive information such as reliability data and validity studies, and to consider the extent of training required to use them and their usefulness for instructional or intervention planning. (See Elliot, Busse, & Gresham, 1993, and McCloskey, 1990, for guidelines for reviewing and selecting rating scales.)

If rating scales are to be used to make important assessment decisions such as referral for in-depth evaluation, their outcomes should be confirmed by other forms of assessment such as direct observation or clinical interviews (Elliot, Busse, & Gresham, 1993).

FORMAL OBSERVATION SCHEDULES

Observational systems are developed to help observers collect and quantify information using systematic specified procedures and recording schedules. Use of such procedures helps make the information gained from observation more manageable. Useful observation systems include

- Category or sign systems that clearly define target behaviors and are exhaustive of the behaviors to be observed
- Procedures for sampling behavior, such as time or event sampling
- Standard recording formats
- Procedures for determining reliability
- Studies documenting reliability and validity

Users tally or mark the occurrence of or frequency with which behaviors occur in predetermined categories during each observation unit, such as every 30 seconds or every minute. If categories are exhaustive, nonoverlapping, and well defined (see Unit VI) and if recording procedures are clearly defined, formal observation systems can be efficient and reliable, and can enhance the quantification of observational data. The development of such observational systems is a major focus of this text.

Formal observation systems have many advantages. They can be used to gain in-depth understanding of many aspects of social and learning behavior. They also can be used repeatedly over time to assess skill development or the effectiveness of instruction or other forms of intervention. In addition, the use of published systems helps facilitate communication among individuals using the same system (Bramlett & Barnett, 1993).

The use of formal observational systems does not eliminate all problems. Since the use of formal schedules focuses the observer's attention on targeted behaviors or events, observers may miss other important behaviors or may not be able to capture the flow of behavior. Also, the amount of training required to use many systems may be extensive. Despite these limitations, observational systems can provide sophisticated and valid accounts of a wide range of observable behaviors. (Locating existing observation systems unfortunately is not easy. A number of useful resources may be found in the Bibliography.)

There is a place for each of these forms of observation in learning settings. Often more than one mode of observing can be used, in a complementary manner. For example, a specimen record, a checklist, and a formal observational schedule might be successively employed over time in addressing a particular observational problem. It is important to use information gathered from multiple methods by key individuals in a child's life to grasp a full picture of the child's behavior. Gathering information from multiple sources over time helps ensure a solid foundation for making valid decisions and planning appropriate learning experiences. Indeed, flexibility in using an array of observational techniques can be the hallmark of the skillful early childhood observer. The issues of validity, reliability, and sampling behavior discussed in later units apply as well to the multiple observation formats discussed in this unit.

The Selective Nature of Our Observations

Each person presented with the task of making specific observations should be able to observe objectively with minimal interference from subjective frames of reference. Obviously, however, the subjective is always going to be a factor—we choose to pay attention to certain things or activities while we ignore others. It is impossible to observe everything in a given situation at the same time; while we are focusing on some attributes of a situation, we are naturally missing others.

To help you become acquainted with your own current approach to observing situations, try this task.

TASK 1: OBSERVATIONS OF YOUR PRESENT SETTING

Observe the setting in which you find yourself. Record your observations, using the Task 1 Worksheet. If others are in the room with you, ask them to engage in the same task. Record your observations in the order in which they are made. Limit the time for the task to 5 minutes.

Then compare your observations with those made by others in the same setting. Include in this comparison:

- The observations made (what you and others selected to observe)
- In what sequence your observations were made and how the sequence of your observations compares with that of others.

Then consider these questions:

- How did you choose what to view?
- Did you employ a strategy for observing the setting? If so, what strategy?
- How did the format of the task influence the nature of your observations?

Task 1 Worksheet

Observations of Your Present Setting (5-Minute Time Limit)

Setting:_____

Time of Day:_____

Observer:_____

Observations in Sequence

  1.

  2.

  3.

  4.

  5.

  6.

  7.

  8.

  9.

10.

Given in the Appendix is a set of sample responses made by three observers in the same setting. Compare your responses with these.

Although it is interesting to note the similarity in responses among the three observers as they viewed the same setting, this example illustrates the selective nature of observing a setting, both in terms of what is observed and the order in which the observations are made.

SUBJECTIVITY IN OBSERVATION

By now it is apparent that a wide range of observations is possible, given the same setting and time, depending on the selectivity of the viewer. The selective and *subjective* nature of what we see is a reflection of many psychological factors, such as previous observation in that setting, our attitudinal framework, our momentary feelings and mood, and any systems of classification we may have for viewing the world, which can be an indication of our interests and occupation.

For example, when an early childhood specialist observes the child of a family friend playing with a puzzle, the child's behaviors are likely to be compared with known developmental milestones gained through reading and past experiences.

TASK 2: OBSERVATIONS OF A SUPERMARKET SCENE

For Task 2, view the photograph of a supermarket scene and make your observations, attempting to take the point of view of the manager of the store and then that of a shopper. Again, limit yourself to 5 minutes for each observation. Record your observations on the Task 2 Worksheet.

Next, compare the content and order in which the observations were made given the two different orientations. Consider (1) in what ways they are the same and how they are different and (2) why you think these differences have occurred.

Certainly, the differing orientations of the store manager and the shopper for observing the supermarket will influence the kinds of observations that are made. The manager, interested in the level

Task 2 Worksheet

Observations of a Supermarket Scene

Observations in Sequence

Manager of Store	Shopper in Store
1.	1.
2.	2.
3.	3.
4.	4.
5.	5.
6.	6.
7.	7.
8.	8.
9.	9.
10.	10.

of business and the related satisfaction of customers, would focus on the number of shoppers; the number and nature of items in shopping carts; the orderliness of the shelves, counters, and aisles; the freshness and movement of items on display; and indications of the efficiency and helpfulness of staff. On the other hand, the shopper would probably focus observations on the cost and variety of items available. As is the manager, but for other reasons, the shopper would be interested in the cleanliness of the store, the orderliness of the aisles, the apparent freshness of produce, and so on. Our needs and points of view influence what we see.

Some other questions that could be posed giving focus to observation in supermarkets include: What produce do people buy? How many customers use shopping lists? How many customers (any individual entering the store) are in the store at various time periods?

AIMING FOR OBJECTIVITY IN OUR OBSERVATIONS

Tasks 1 and 2 demonstrate the *selective* nature of our perceptions. Such selectivity is natural because the process of perception demands

Task 2. A Supermarket Scene

selectivity. When we are observing in order to make decisions or to draw conclusions, it is necessary to be *objective*, to have a focus so that our observations are purposeful and defined. Therefore, we must consider such questions as "What are we going to view?" and "For what purpose?" Such questions increase the objectivity of the observations that we make. The following guidelines are given to help you differentiate objective from subjective observations.

- Objective observations (factors or details others could readily agree on):

    The number of chairs, tables, windows, and so forth, in a room
    The color of objects
    The size of objects relative to one to another
    Behavior as it occurs (but not interpreting this behavior)

- Subjective observations (unique perceptions, biases, or individual points of view that others might not agree with):

    A statement about perceived conditions, such as "This room is hot" (it may not seem hot to others)
    The physical attractiveness of a room
    Personal characteristics of the people in a setting, such as "She looks pretty"

It is possible to carry the quest for objectivity to the point of absurdity: "The walls of the room are painted light yellow, shade #428 ACME Opaque paint, and the air temperature in the room is 72.4 degrees Fahrenheit." Under most conditions, this degree of precision would be unnecessary.

TASK 3: DISTINGUISHING OBJECTIVE FROM SUBJECTIVE OR INTERPRETIVE OBSERVATIONS

Go back to the record of observations you made for Task 1 and consider which of your reactions conveyed *specific* and *objective* information, and which involved subjective observations, employing the guidelines just given. Label each of your observations or interpretations "objective" or "subjective" in the margin of your worksheet.

If your observations tended to fall heavily in the subjective category, you have an indication of your natural tendency to view situations subjectively. There is nothing wrong with making subjective comments so long as the observer is aware of the subjectivity and

this is reflected in the use of qualified language: "The air feels cold"—
not "The air is cold."

An additional dilemma that faces the observer is the tendency to
make inferences or draw conclusions from scanty evidence not necessarily supported by other data. Thus, if you noted that a girl sitting to
your left appeared to be happy and what you actually saw was a girl with
a smile on her face, you might be drawing an inappropriate conclusion
on the basis of evidence—the smile might hide disdain, discomfort, or
boredom.

THE EFFECT OF THE OBSERVER'S PRESENCE

Look at the pictures of a classroom in Figures 4.1 and 4.2. They
illustrate the effect of an outside observer's presence, in this case with
a camera, on the spontaneous flow of behavior in a given setting. The
first photograph was taken immediately upon the observer's entrance
into the classroom; Figure 4.2 was taken several seconds later while the

FIGURE 4.1. School Classroom

FIGURE 4.2. Classroom after Photographer Enters

observer (with camera) stood by the doorway of the room. In Figure 4.2 the child in the striped shirt on the right has responded to the observer. This illustrates how the presence of a photographer, or any observer, can influence the nature of some behaviors that occur as part of the ongoing sequence within that setting.

However, it has been noted that, in general, the effect of the presence of the outside observer on pupil behavior tends to decrease over time (Masling & Stern, 1969). With this in mind, it is important to note that the observer, if he or she is new to a setting, should be within that setting on several occasions prior to making systematic observations or drawing conclusions based on those observations.

DRAWING INFERENCES

Until now our emphasis has been on objective observing. However, such an emphasis is not intended to negate the importance of drawing inferences as a result of the observation process. Inferences can generate ideas—hypotheses to be checked against other evidence, and, potentially, creative solutions to problems. Thus, inferences about another person's feelings ("Linda appears to be a happy child," or "Michael seems to be a bright, well-adjusted child"), supported by a variety of observational data such as facial expressions and the content of conversations over a period of time, can lead to certain conclusions made or actions taken in the classroom, on the job, at home, or in relationships with others.

Though we will not move into a philosophical discussion here, it is essential that we now consider the nature of various inferences that are commonly made in education settings. Each day educators make statements such as:

Molly is a creative child.
Anthony isn't very bright.
The boys in this room are hostile and aggressive.
José is not distractible and attends well during class.
Andrea has a very poor self-concept.

Psychological phenomena such as creativity, intelligence, aggressiveness, distractibility, and self-concept are not directly observable. Rather, these labels or descriptions are applied on the basis of observable behaviors that represent commonly agreed upon indicators of the constructs just noted.

Although all of us make inferences about others each day, few of us are aware of the way observations provide support for such inferences. Take the example of "self-concept." What do we mean when we refer to a child's good or poor self-concept? We need to raise such questions as: What observational data can be used to support the inferences and conclusions drawn? Would another person arrive at the same conclusions? How many instances of particular observable behaviors are necessary before we are willing to state that a child has a poor self-concept? (Sampling and the systematic collection of observational data to lend support to inferences are topics dealt with at length in Unit VIII.)

Let's consider the role of observations in making inferences with the following example.

TASK 4: OBSERVATIONS OF A GIRL IN A HEAD START CLASSROOM

For Task 4, look at the photograph of a girl in a Head Start classroom and consider what objective statements could be made about her and what inferences might be drawn about her behavior in the context of the activity and classroom.

Task 4 Worksheet

Observations of a Girl in a Head Start Classroom

Observations Made	Inferences Drawn	Observations Supporting Inferences (#1, #2)
1.	A.	A.
2.	B.	B.
3.	C.	C.
4.	D.	D.
5.	E.	E.

The following information will help clarify the situation:

> The girl and the other children are 4 years old and have attended Head Start for two months.
> The children are engaged in free play, which generally continues for about 30 minutes.
> The girl has been sitting in the same place without making any sounds for at least five minutes.

Using the Task 4 Worksheet, indicate possible inferences about the girl's behavior in the classroom, supporting your statements with objective observational data. Indicate by corresponding letters which observations are the basis for your inferences.

Review your list of inferences about the little girl in the picture and their supportive observations. Then consider the possible observations and inferences for Task 4 given in the Appendix.

In making observations and inferences in most situations, we have the benefit of viewing the flux of behavior over time. A single photograph obviously presents a static moment in time, making it essential

Task 4. Girl in a Head Start Classroom

that the viewer question what actually preceded that momentary instance. Prior to the situation depicted in the picture shown in Task 4, the girl might have been actively involved in play with the boys in the block area, or she might have just sat down after playing with a group of children in the dollhouse area. If the viewer cannot obtain such information about prior activities, care should be exercised about drawing strong inferences. The strength of inferences depends on the prevalence or the frequency of the observed behavior that supports the inference. Sampling behavior over time and across activities eliminates the tendency to draw inferences on the basis of scanty observational data.

Yet the hunches of teachers and caregivers gained through observation are very important. The "ahas" can be followed up, and the insights gained over time are essential for developing more systematic techniques of observation that can guide appropriate interventions.

Defining the Problem and Describing the Setting

By now it should be apparent that making useful and objective observations is a complex task. The classification of child behaviors and the organization of tasks and the physical components of the setting can facilitate the objective observation process, as well as the communication of findings to others. The type of grouping or classification used must relate to the particular focus or concern of the observer. For example, a kindergarten teacher interested in developing appropriate concept materials for a class would focus on a child's use (across activities) of the particular concepts being developed, while ignoring the child's social interaction with others. On the other hand, if the teacher wanted to develop a program that encouraged social interaction among children, focus would be placed on ways of classifying social patterns in the classroom.

In this unit we seek to develop a systematic approach to structuring observations so that enough data can be gathered to realize the goals for which observation techniques were used in the first place. Given the inherent selectivity in the observation process, and the need for objectivity discussed earlier, agreement between individuals on the specific foci of observation is essential. Although ways by which the reliability of observation can be increased will be considered in the next three units, it is essential at this point to develop an approach that can do the following:

- Force the observer to clearly define the problem or question he or she wishes to answer through the use of observation techniques.
- Take into account the constraints a given setting (i.e., classroom, daycare, or home) imposes on the scope of potential behaviors, and lead the observer to describe the components of an observational situation, including the overall physical setting, materials available to the individuals within the setting, individuals within the situation, and time of day.
- Take into account the organization of activities, teaching approaches, and teacher–child interactions.

- Provide a system for describing, counting, recording, and categorizing instances of behavior, allowing more than one observer to collect or interpret the same data.
- Recognize that one cannot directly observe emotions, cognition, or attitudes. Rather, these are inferred on the basis of viewing countable, describable instances of behavior over time and in the multiple settings experienced by the child.

DEFINING ONE'S OBSERVATIONAL PURPOSE

The range of questions that might be posed in learning settings and for which observation techniques are appropriate is broad. A curriculum coordinator might be intent on evaluating the influence a new social studies curriculum has on questioning behaviors displayed in the classroom; teachers or psychologists in training might want an overview of the range of typical behaviors exhibited by children from different age groups attending the same school; the school psychologist posed with a referral of a child demonstrating "learning difficulties" might be interested in that child's classroom behavior as he or she interacts with peers, the teacher, and the learning situation; a principal of a large urban school might want to know if pupils receive more feedback on assignments when student teachers are present. Some sample problems that provide focus for the classroom observer follow:

- The teacher will be interested in the number and content of cooperative exchanges between children that occur during the school day. The teacher will be interested in this observation in order to make inferences about the "cooperative behavior" of children in the classroom.
- The teacher, concerned about the performance of John Jones and questioning the appropriateness of a referral to the school psychologist, will want to know if John appears to understand curriculum content, is smaller than other children in the classroom, is very quiet, is inattentive, or does not respond to classroom instructions or directions.
- The principal, concerned about the lack of space in the school, will be interested in how classes make use of space currently allotted.
- The supervisory teacher will be concerned by the extent to which a student teacher is providing practice appropriate to specific goals of the lesson.

- The early childhood teacher will want to understand the skills a child has in relation to the curriculum across developmental areas as well as the approaches and strategies the child uses when engaging in tasks.
- The special educator will want to know not only the skills the blind, deaf, cerebral palsy, physically disabled child has but also how appropriate and adaptive the environment is in meeting the child's needs.
- The early childhood administrator will want to look at the interactive behaviors of teachers and aides with children.
- The daycare administrator will want to make sure the physical, nutritional, cognitive, language, and affective needs of children are addressed.

Posing questions or presenting problems in a form that allows the observer to understand the specific purpose of the intended observations and eventually arrive at an answer to the posed question is essential. For example, the question "Are the pupils in this class motivated to engage in shared storybook reading?" in its current form is insufficiently defined to focus the observer on specific behaviors in the setting, because one must ask:

What is motivation?
Can motivation be observed directly?
What, in specific behavioral terms, is "engaging" in shared story-
     book reading?

Here the observer must consider what is involved in shared storybook reading. For example, what books are used? What activities does the teacher use to involve children? What kinds of questions does the teacher ask? More directly answered questions include:

What does the teacher do to encourage child participation during
     shared storybook reading?
How does the teacher encourage children to elaborate on their
     responses?

These questions limit the observer to directly observable behavior—specific behaviors on the part of the teacher—and do not deal with motivation, which can be inferred only from a variety of observed behaviors, such as the child's responding to the book-sharing activity illustrated in Figure 5.1.

FIGURE 5.1. Girl Responds to Book-Sharing Activity

TASK 5: DIFFERENTIATING CLEARLY STATED FROM POORLY STATED QUESTIONS

As a further exercise, determine which of the questions given on the Task 5 Worksheet are clearly stated. Check the appropriate column for each question and fill in the reason for your response. When you have completed this task, compare your answers with the sample responses about each question given in the Appendix.

THE CHARACTERISTICS OF THE SETTING

After one defines the purpose for observation, a careful analysis of the setting itself is needed in order to develop appropriate categories for observation. The general setting characteristically dictates the nature of behaviors that can be observed in that situation and the kinds of activities that can take place. For example, a child's verbal interactions with adults cannot be observed if that setting is restricted to children. It is also important to focus on those aspects of the setting that can limit, direct, or facilitate behavior. These factors include:

Task 5 Worksheet

Differentiating Clearly Stated from Poorly Stated Questions

Question	Well Stated	Poorly Stated	Reason
1. Are boys more restless than girls during small-group "big book" activities?			
2. Does the teacher in this classroom encourage questioning behavior?			
3. During a given kindergarten class day, how many individual children choose to look at a book during free play?			
4. Why do the girls in the kindergarten class appear to be more motivated to clean up after snack time?			

- Amount of physical space available
- People in the setting who will differ along the dimensions of age, sex, and role
- Tangible materials in the setting and their placement
- General physical characteristics of the setting itself such as temperature, lighting, room size, and organization of space
- Organization of activity areas
- Appropriateness of materials and arrangements for children with handicapping conditions

The organization of space into activity areas, the type and placement of materials, and teacher philosophy and approach to presenting instructional materials, along with teacher behaviors, all interact with child learning characteristics and styles. For example, Morrow (1991) found in a study of kindergarten classrooms that there was a significant relationship between literacy materials displayed and the frequency of children's literacy-related behaviors during free play. The goal, therefore, is to identify the environmental factors that potentially can affect the child's behavior. Aspects of these factors will be developed in later sections of this unit.

An overview of the total setting is helpful in developing an understanding of the situation, but it is also important to reemphasize the selective nature of observing behavior. An individual will ignore those portions of a setting where little activity is occurring and will focus on areas of the setting where the central activity is taking place.

The influence of a setting on the behavior of an individual can be illustrated from another perspective. For example:

How does the same child interact with others in the classroom, in the gym, on the playground, in the neighborhood, and at home?

How does the factory worker interact with other workers during rest periods, in the cafeteria, and on the job itself?

Barker (1968) made a useful point in his exposition of the mutual relationship between people and their environment. The environment, or context of behavior, has its own structures (boundaries, physical and temporal attributes) that limit or dictate the individual's behavior. A child's behavior on the playground is different from that in the classroom; on the playground the child is more likely to run and shout than in the classroom. A doctor generally functions differently on the golf course than in the hospital; on the golf course the doctor's behavior resembles that of other golfers, while in the hospital it is like that of other doctors. Clearly, the setting makes a great difference in the doctor's behavior. Thus, the interrelationship between an individual and a setting generates an important question: What characterizes the behavior of the same person in different situations or settings? (Barker and Wright's *One Boy's Day*, 1951, provides stimulating reading in this area.)

Pursuing this point further, particularly with younger children, we might consider a child's behavior separately in different activity areas of the room, such as the housekeeping corner, work tables, the block area, the book shelf, or the painting area. With older pupils, we might consider behaviors as displayed in different subject-matter classrooms or curricular periods. In summary then, the observer must take into account the various influences of settings that limit or provide opportunities for the behaviors of individuals within those settings. Smith and Connolly (1980) and Moore (1987) provide research about the many features of the environment that influence both child behavior and teacher opinions.

TASK 6: CONSTRAINTS IMPOSED BY THE SETTING

Considering our analysis of influences on possible behaviors imposed by the setting, look at the photograph of a playground setting. Using the Task 6 Worksheet, list those characteristics of the people within this setting that might restrict behavior. Speculate on some possible behaviors that probably could not occur because of these constraints and on some behaviors that would be facilitated by these same factors. Next, consider in what ways the available "materials" (play equipment) and the amount of space on the playground tend to produce some general constraints and in what ways they facilitate certain kinds of behavior. Compare your responses with the sample responses given in the Appendix.

ANALYZING THE COMPONENTS OF THE SETTING

Further considerations in viewing the contexts in which one observes behavior are components such as the physical setting, tangible materials of the setting, individuals within the setting, and the interactions that take place between adults and children. Each of these components is described in the following sections and practice in observing them is given in the accompanying tasks.

Task 6 Worksheet

Constraints Imposed by the Setting

Category	Characteristics	Unlikely Behaviors	Likely Behaviors
1. People			
2. Materials Available			
3. Space			
4. Other Features (indicate)			

57

TASK 6. **A Playground Setting**

Observing and Describing the Overall Physical Setting

Unlike human behavior, which undergoes considerable change over time, the physical setting in which we observe behavior usually remains quite stable. When observing, one should consider the physical characteristics of the situation, such as the temperature of a room and its implications for the kinds of behavior to be expected in that room, the amount of space provided in the setting for a range of activities, and the nature of artificial and natural lighting and its placement within a setting.

Observing and Describing Tangible Materials

Tangible materials might be considered next because they are often central to the behavioral activities in a setting. Such materials include large pieces of equipment (desks, climbing and other playground equipment, sandbox) as well as expendable materials (paper, book, pencils, puzzles, and teacher-designed materials).

In addition to identifying and describing these materials in isolation, it is important to note the cultural relevance of materials and the arrangement or organization of these materials by people within the setting to meet their particular goals. For example, the larger setting might be organized into activity areas, such as seat activities, library corner, science area, or arts and crafts area (as illustrated in the photograph shown in Figure 5.2).

Observing and Describing Individuals Within the Setting

A third major component of our analysis of the setting in which behaviors are observed is a description of the individuals within that setting. Task 7 provides practice in doing this.

TASK 7: VISIBLE CHARACTERISTICS OF INDIVIDUALS

Look at the Task 7 photograph on the next page and write down your descriptions of the *visible* characteristics of each individual pictured, using the Task 7 Worksheet. As you will notice, the Task 7 Worksheet lists only characteristics that are *directly observable*. In making descriptions, one should not feel compelled to make inferences about emotions, social backgrounds, current roles, and so on, of these individuals. To do so would be an example of how often we draw conclusions and make judgments about individuals based on characteristics that are beyond what we actually can see. (See Kleinmuntz, 1967, pp. 92–109, for a detailed discussion of observing expressive behavior.)

FIGURE 5.2. **Kindergarten Classroom**

Task 7 Worksheet

Visible Characteristics of Individuals

Category	Boy	Girl	Adult
1. Approximate Age			
2. Sex			
3. Physical Features—color of hair, clothing, body build, height, glasses			
4. Movement and Gestures			
5. Physical Handicaps			

An observer interested in a subset of children (such as the younger children in the group), or only one child, has more flexibility for description than would be possible in a larger group. Obviously, in a classroom group of 20 children, it is impossible for the observer to focus careful attention on more than one child at a time. Therefore, if the observer is interested in describing the physical characteristics of an entire group of children, it is necessary to employ a technique that allows for sys-

TASK 7. **Three Individuals**

tematic ordering of observations of the group, viewing one member of the group at a time.

It is important to emphasize that we are observing individuals at this point without considering their behavior and without considering the ways in which they interact with each other, physically or verbally. After describing the individuals whose behavior is of interest to you, it is helpful to take notice of some general characteristics of the group of people within the setting. Such *summarizing characteristics* include:

Number of individuals present
Ratio of boys to girls
Ratio of adults to children
Number of cultural and/or racial groups represented
Number of children with handicapping conditions

Observing Adult–Child Interactions

The fourth component of our analysis of the setting is the interactions that occur within the setting between adults (teachers, assistants, parents, other professionals) and children. These interactions are of paramount importance for the classroom observer. For example, how the teacher presents instruction—introducing different genres of children's books; asking open-ended questions versus labeling—will influence children's behaviors and learning outcomes. The teacher or other classroom observer will want to observe those interactions that research has indicated are important for learning. (For further details, see, for example, the guidelines for developmentally appropriate practice specified by Bredekamp, 1987; Good & Brophy, 1991; and Ysseldyke, Christenson, & Thurlow, 1987.) These interactions include the ways in which adults

Manage disruptive behavior
Use techniques to motivate children and help them stay engaged
Communicate expectations
Serve as language and communication models
Encourage thinking
Are able to break down tasks into their component parts
Provide feedback and praise
Encourage children to engage in new behaviors
Organize and present curricular activities
Use consistent routines

THE CONTEXT OF BEHAVIOR

In this unit we have isolated the key components of a setting that should be considered when observing. In an attempt to illustrate the ways in which physical features of a setting—the objects and the people within that setting—combine to produce the context of observed behavior, we present an example of observing the library of an elementary school. The time is the library period for second-grade pupils. For this observation, we want to take note of the physical features of the room, the objects in it, and the people and their activities, and include a list of summarizing characteristics.

To help us in our observation, we have made a diagram of the exact layout of the library setting (see Figure 5.3). Here the exact seating positions can be indicated and the activity areas detailed. Such diagrams are also useful in understanding physical constraints, which might hamper movement or might be impossible for a physically handicapped child. If a particular child is of concern, diagrams can be made with arrows used to show the direction and nature of the interaction of the target child with peers.

In Figure 5.4, we have listed the key components of the library setting. As shown, the observed activity is a result of the interplay of people with their setting. Now do Task 8, using the example in Figure 5.4 as a model. Pick a similar setting.

TASK 8: KEY COMPONENTS OF A SETTING

Analyze the components of a setting. Distinguish physical features, objects, and people, and name the activities taking place. Write your responses on the Task 8 Worksheet. Summarize the characteristics of the setting and activities that take place. Then, focusing on the constraints imposed by the setting, make predictions about what kinds of behavior are likely to occur. Do you find that these predictions more or less correspond to the observed activities?

We have stressed the importance of observing and describing the environmental contexts in which classroom behaviors occur in order to generate an awareness of facilitating and constraining influences. In describing environments, it is important to remember that the classroom is constantly changing—another adult can enter the room, class groupings change with the curriculum, a particular child is absent, and so forth. Since behavior is always determined to some extent by the

FIGURE 5.3. **Diagram of Library**

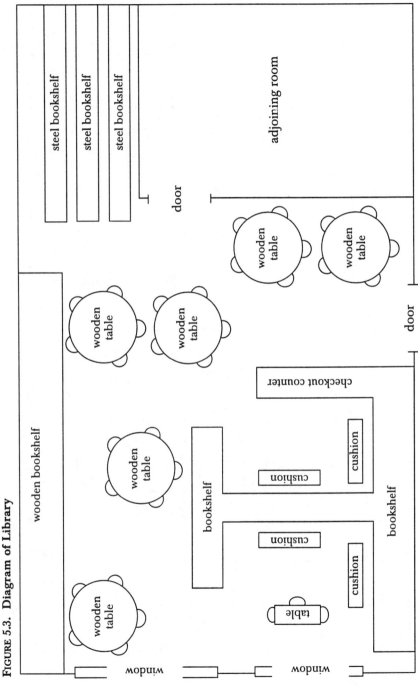

FIGURE 5.4. Key Components of a Setting

Setting: Elementary school library
Time: Library period for second-grade pupils

Physical Features	Objects	People	Activities
Rectangular room	Three rows of steel bookshelves	One young girl in a blue dress	Copying a drawing from a magazine
Yellow colored walls	Two wooden bookshelves against walls		
One large glass window	One T-shaped low bookshelf separating 2 areas with cushions	One middle-aged woman in a green dress	Often coming out from adjoining room with a paper in hand
One small glass window			Checks the paper with the girl
One adjoining room with a window door	One green and two yellow chairs with a small rectangular table in one corner		Goes back to her room
One big door leading into library	Six round tables, "natural wood," each with five chairs	Two young boys in the rows of bookshelves	Searching for books
Checkout counter	Index card boxes		
Overhead fluorescent light turned on	Books on the counter	Three young girls sitting at one of the round tables	Two girls talking with each other while pointing to a picture in a book; one girl looking at book in front of her
Carpeted floor	Books on the shelves		
	Duplicating machine		
	Painting of a man		
	Three plants		
	Paper slips, pins, stamps on the counter		
	Bulletin board		
	Large cushions on the floor		

Summarizing Characteristics:
• Presence of only six students in the library suggests that only small groups of second-grade pupils use the library at a time, not the entire class, because, at the time of the observation, only the six students were there, although there was ample room for a class.
• All individuals present seem occupied.

Task 8 Worksheet

Key Components of a Setting

Setting:

Time:

Physical Features	Objects	People	Activities

Summarizing Characteristics:

environment in which it occurs, it is sometimes important to describe the shifts within the environment.

It should be emphasized that the study of the environment per se and of the relationship between individuals and their settings has been a central focus of the field of ecological psychology as discussed in Unit II. A complex network of theoretical constructs, empirical findings, and field methods has resulted from the ecologist's perspective. The purpose of this unit has been to highlight some components of a complex study of "behavior settings" that can be useful to the early childhood observer.

Labeling and Categorizing Behavior

The term *behavior* has been used earlier in this book, but we have not defined it precisely because our focus has been on other aspects of the complex observation process. In order to consider dimensions for labeling behavior, let us define *behavior* as any observable, overt action or activity that an individual exhibits in a setting. Behaviors range from solitary, nonvocal activity (sitting in a chair, looking out the window) to verbal and nonverbal interaction with others (a fist fight and verbal exchange between two third-graders on the playground). When referring to constructs such as "self-concept," which we cannot directly observe, we are dealing with an inference or conclusion that may be based on observable behaviors.

DIMENSIONS FOR LABELING BEHAVIORS

Within education and the behavioral sciences one can select from a variety of measures, checklists, rating scales, and categories for viewing behavior in the classroom (see Bibliography). Recently, the variety of efforts to measure behavior have reflected a behavioral analysis orientation. The resulting instruments have focused on the teacher's verbal behavior as well as on a wide range of verbal and nonverbal pupil responses, and have in general been devised in a manner consistent with purposes of the particular researchers. Although we advocate a perspective that places behavior within the context of its setting and that underscores the importance of making qualitative judgments, inferences, and decisions on the basis of observation data, we also advocate an approach that allows us to consider behavior from various points of view. Consequently, a cognitive-developmental psychologist might make inferences about the level of a child's cognitive-intellectual functioning on the basis of observing behaviors defined as related to cognitive functioning. On the other hand, an early childhood educator might make inferences about the age-appropriateness of certain social behaviors as a result of observing children interact in a kindergarten situation and his or her knowledge of developmental expectations for children from diverse cultural and linguistic backgrounds. Furthermore, inferences about a child's emotional maturity and level of affective expression might be drawn from observing behaviors that theoretically are considered attributes of a given emotion. Our approach allows the observer, whatever his or her philosophical stance or professional role, to employ direct observation for the kind of analyses and interventions that he or she thinks are most appropriate.

Despite the dogmatism of many developers of observation techniques, it is important to remember that observation systems differ in the extent to which they can be applied or generalized to situations other than those for which they were designed or developed (Kerlinger, 1973). Therefore, it becomes the burden of every observer, having defined his or her purpose, to determine the appropriateness of a particular observation system or series of behavioral categories. To help the reader evaluate a particular system, we will raise a number of issues that should be considered in evaluating observation systems and in deciding which approach to use for sampling behavior.

Knowing and Defining Behaviors

Since most observation approaches and systems are designed for particular research or educational purposes, the developers of these systems focus on those behaviors related to the objectives of their particular project. For example:

- A researcher interested in observing a teacher's questioning behavior should consider all the types of questioning behavior that are conceivable in classrooms.
- A teacher interested in observing the "hyperactivity" of a particular child needs some understanding of behaviors that are representative of hyperactivity.

Thus, observing human behavior requires some knowledge of that behavior (Kerlinger, 1973). It would not be possible for a novice to observe systematically a doctor's operating room behavior without some understanding of the procedures employed. From this knowledge base it becomes possible to list potential categories for observation.

In their overview of various observation systems, Simon and Boyer (1967) employed a major distinction between affective and cognitive observational systems. The individual interested in studying the classroom's emotional climate and "how it [the classroom] is conditioned by teacher reactions to pupil's feeling, ideas, work efforts, or actions" (p. viii) would use an affective system. If, however, the individual were more concerned with studying verbal patterns in the classroom or in children's problem-solving techniques, a cognitive system would be more appropriate. The *Mirrors for Behavior* series (Simon & Boyer, 1967, 1970, 1974) provides a more detailed characterization of these two generalized category systems, with examples of different classroom observation systems. (Unfortunately, this resource has not been recently updated.)

Once the observer has defined the problems or question, the observations must be structured so that they can be

- Communicated in an organized fashion to another individual who was not present, such as another teacher or a parent
- Generated in a manner similar to those of another observer viewing the same behaviors at the same time

MUTUALLY EXCLUSIVE AND EXHAUSTIVE CATEGORIES

Mutually Exclusive Categories

In order to eliminate confusion as to which observed behaviors are to be recorded in which categories, and to increase reliability (see Unit VII), it is essential that clear definitions of behavior be indicated so that each category of observable behavior is precisely distinguishable and independent from other categories (i.e., is mutually exclusive). "Asking a question" and "making a statement" are mutually exclusive categories, for a person can engage in only one of these behaviors at the same point in time. Other examples of mutually exclusive categories are standing and sitting, driving and swimming.

If the observer has difficulty deciding whether an observed behavior belongs in one category rather than another because of overlapping definitions of those categories, the classifications are not mutually exclusive and need refinement. For example, "using correct grammar" and "asking a question" are not mutually exclusive categories. In this example, if a pupil asks a question and the question is grammatically correct, the observer would have difficulty categorizing that observation. (On another count, from the point of view of clear definition, the first of these categories would have to be specified so that observers would know what is meant to be "grammatically correct.") Task 9 provides practice in distinguishing examples of mutually exclusive categories.

TASK 9: DISTINGUISHING MUTUALLY EXCLUSIVE CATEGORIES

In the examples given on the Task 9 Worksheet, indicate whether the clusters of categories are mutually exclusive or overlapping. Then check your responses with the sample responses in the Appendix.

Setting Limits

As the observer defines the basic problem or area of interest for observing, it is necessary to set limits on the universe of behaviors to be observed. For example, an individual interested in studying "teaching behavior in the classroom" must delimit a problem area to provide focus, such as studying types of teacher questions, categorizing teacher statements, or counting the number of approvals by teachers to pupil responses. If the observer chose to focus on types of teacher questions, all other behaviors would be ignored, and the observer would attend only to questioning behavior—that is, the universe of behavior. Furthermore, if the observer were interested in studying teacher questioning behavior in the classroom, the categories would have to subsume the total range of possible behaviors that constitute teacher questioning behavior.

Task 9 Worksheet

Distinguishing Mutually Exclusive Categories

Categories	Mutually Exclusive	Overlapping

1. running
    lying prone
    sitting in place
    standing in place		

2. laughing
    crying
    talking		

3. reading
    looking
    listening		

4. asking a question
    giving a command
    stating an opinion		

For example, the teacher asks for

Specific fact
Definition
Opinion
Clarification or elaboration
Application
Evaluation

Making Categories Exhaustive

The categories established must be exhaustive in that every possible instance of observed questioning behavior (or every behavior in the universe being considered) can be classified in one of the available categories. As Kerlinger (1973) has noted, the universe of behaviors that the observer considers can vary in scope depending on the objectives of the observation process or the question being asked. Task 10 provides practice in establishing exhaustive categories.

TASK 10: ESTABLISHING EXHAUSTIVE CATEGORIES

Develop an exhaustive series of categories for the following defined universe of behavior:

Large-muscle coordination (gross motor skills) as exhibited by 4- to 6-year-olds during playground activities.

In developing your list of categories, you should consider the following questions:

What is an operational definition of large-motor coordination?
Is the problem as stated precise enough to avoid considering behaviors other than "large-muscle coordination" as observed on the playground?

List the categories on the Task 10 Worksheet.

As you may have noticed, there is some degree of ambiguity as to what constitutes large-muscle coordination. Therefore, you might have asked for a clearer definition, such as "a child exhibiting behavior on the playground requiring use of the legs, arms, head, and/or body." By excluding manipulations with hands, fingers, and toes, we eliminate fine-motor skills from the definition. If you are working with a motorically handicapped child, it will be necessary to specify "large-motor coordination" in greater detail.

As you might see when comparing your list of categories with that of the sample responses given in the Appendix, an indepen-

Task 10 Worksheet

Categories of Large-Muscle Coordination Playground Activity

1.   6.

2.   7.

3.   8.

4.   9.

5.   10.

---

dent observer employing your list of categories might observe a behavior that could not be categorized on your list. Therefore, employing an "other" category in the development of your observation schedule would allow the list of categories to be refined at a later observation session. For example, in using the list presented as a sample response, how would a child's activity on a teeter-totter be classified? This would have to be classified in the "other" category because there is no appropriate category. If the "other" list began to have a large number of tallies, it would be necessary to refine the original listing to be more comprehensive.

SPECIFYING CATEGORIES

In devising categories and defining behaviors, one also must consider the specificity of what one actually observes. It must be determined whether very narrow, easily observed, specific behavior units or broader chunks of behavior are more useful in answering the observation question. For example, considering displays of affective behavior in the classroom, one could note the number of times a child smiles during an hour, as well as to whom these smiles are directed and/or under what conditions, or the number of grimaces in a given time period. Or an observer could more broadly categorize affective behavior in terms of the percentage of time a child spent in interactive play. The broader category "interactive play" encompasses a wide range of discrete behaviors.

When individual observers employ a system of narrowly defined categories, their consistency and agreement in classifying behaviors is likely to be high. By reducing the behaviors to be observed to such detail, the observer also greatly reduces the degree of inference introduced into the observation processes, eliminating subjectivity to a greater extent than when broader, more global categories are employed. However, if the behavioral units become too discrete—finger tapping or counts of eyeblinks—the observer may have difficulty making generalizations or "abstracting" from these observations, and the observations can become meaningless data for the teacher (though they might not be for an experimental psychologist).

> When categories are narrow → observer agreement is high → the degree of inference is low → generalizations are more difficult to make → subjectivity is low.

On the other hand, if very broad categories are used, more difficulty is encountered in achieving agreement between observers. Using the category "anxious behavior" versus "nonanxious behavior," the lack of specificity allows much leeway for subjective interpretations of the meaning of these categories. Is a twitching foot classified as an example of anxious behavior? Broader categories that lack definition or specificity require the observer to make more subjective interpretations of observed behavior before classifying an observation into a given category. Although reliability is decreased by employing broader categories, the observer may be making a more meaningful and useful interpretation of the problem at hand.

> When categories are broad → observer agreement is low → the degree of inference is high → generalizations are easier to come by → subjectivity is high.

The learner of observation skills should aim at a minimum degree of inference: Categories that are too vague allow different observers to place different interpretations on the same behavior; categories that are too specific, although they cut down ambiguity and unreliability, are often too rigid and inflexible for easy application.

CATEGORY AND SIGN SYSTEMS

From another perspective, Medley and Mitzel (1963) discuss two approaches to the construction of items for an observation schedule. The first approach, called a *category system*, requires the observer to list a set of categories such that every observed behavior can be recorded into one, and only one, of a series of mutually exclusive categories. For example, Flanders (1965, 1975) devised a classic schedule listing 10 types of verbal behavior that might conceivably occur in the classroom. Using the Flanders system, every utterance of the teacher or pupil can be classified.

As another example, we can make our own list of mutually exhaustive categories for a particular situation. If we were to investigate the nature of interactive play at the preschool level, we would list mutually exclusive and exhaustive categories of interaction. On a recording format similar to the Category System Sample Worksheet (Figure 6.1), one could list the categories, using as many columns as necessary for the number of children being observed. The sample given is an observation of interactive play among preschool children. Since child behaviors often vary across activities and settings (context), it is important to indicate the context on recording forms, such as that presented in Figure 6.1. If the observer wishes to document development over time or the effects of intervention, it is important as well to indicate the dates of observation on recording formats. If all the recording is to be done on the same date, the date can be indicated on the top of the form. If it is to be carried out over time, it should be indicated next to the observed

FIGURE 6.1. **Category System Sample Worksheet**
   Interactive Peer Play

Category	Child A		Child B		Child C	
	Date	Context	Date	Context	Date	Context
Solitary play						
Parallel play						
Interactive play with one child						
Interactive play with more than one child						
Looking around only						

behavior. Different colored pens can be used if desired to code different dates.

The observer using such a system records and *categorizes* every behavior that each individual child demonstrates. The record of observations for a given time period shows the total number of units of behavior observed and their frequency classified into each category for each child and over the entire group sampled.

In contrast, a *sign system* involves listing beforehand a limited number of specific kinds of behavior of interest to the observer. During a stated observation time period the record of observations will show which of these behaviors actually occurred and which did not occur. An observer using a sign-system approach records only those behaviors that fall into one of the preconceived categories listed. Presumably, many behaviors would not be recorded at all and would be ignored. Therefore, a sign system includes mutually exhaustive categories, but the categories do not need to be exhaustive. (In some systems these signs are referred to as "events.")

For example, one might be interested in observing rule-following behaviors using a sign system. The Sign System Sample Worksheet (Figure 6.2) gives an observation of students' ability to follow some selected class rules. In using the sign system in this example, the observer has determined the behaviors that indicate following class rules. Using a similar worksheet, the observer would record instances of the students' demonstrating these behaviors. The observer would use as many rows

FIGURE 6.2. **Sign System Sample Worksheet**
Following Selected Class Rules

Date: _____

Observer: _____

Child	Remains in Seat	Raises Hand	Talks in Turn

as necessary for the number of children and as many columns as necessary for the number of behaviors.

Note that here there are no "other" or "etc." categories. Behaviors other than those in a given category would be ignored because they are irrelevant to the purpose of the observation.

In summary, the major distinction between category and sign systems could be characterized as follows:

Category System	Sign System
Every observed behavior must be classified (Exclusive *and* exhaustive categories)	Only *specific* predetermined behaviors are classified (Exclusive, *but not* exhaustive categories)

DEVELOPING CATEGORIES

The following steps may be taken in developing categories that are appropriate to the observational task at hand (these are similar to the steps listed in Unit III for developing checklists and rating scales):

1. *Brainstorming.* Think through all possible approaches to your problem. For example, "Is my observational question clear and specific?" "Can it be answered through observation?" "Are the behaviors I've chosen to observe relevant to my question?"

   Brainstorm the problem with your associates. How do they perceive the behaviors you wish to target? Discuss areas of agreement or differences. This discussion can help lead you to the categories you employ in your observational instrument.

2. *Reviewing.* Survey the literature. How have others approached the same or similar problems? Are their definitions of the target areas complete? What procedures have been used, and what were the outcomes? What stumbling blocks were encountered?

3. *Task-analyzing.* Break down the behavior to be observed into its component parts—engage in a *"task analysis"* (see Gagné, 1985). Ask what sub-behaviors or events make up the targeted domain of behavior. For example, in order to develop categories of verbal communication among preschoolers, one would generate a list of the kinds of verbal behaviors that are possible and would exclude nonverbal behaviors:

   Asking for assistance
   Seeking information (asking a question)

Commanding

Mimicking

Making statements of fact, hope, and so forth

4. *Previewing.* Go into a situation that is representative of the setting in which you will have to observe and generate a running record or describe carefully those behaviors of interest. Consider whether the observation was typical, representative, and adequate. From these observations, hone into your question and abstract the important behaviors or events (see also Martin, 1976).

5. *Field-testing.* Try your system out (with a co-observer, if possible), and revise as necessary.

One could pursue any or all of these activities depending on the difficulty of the categorizing task, previous experience, and one's patience!

Making Reliable Observations: Avoiding Observational Bias

In order for us to have confidence in our observational findings, it is important to consider a number of technical issues. Issues related to reliability will be covered in this unit and issues related to sampling, validity, and using observational outcomes in Unit VIII.

Two types of reliability are essential: Observers need to agree with each other (*agreement reliability*) and to determine whether they have obtained a stable picture of children's behavior across a brief period of time (*stability*). Each of these forms of reliability will be detailed in this unit along with a section that presents challenges to obtaining reliable observations.

INCREASING OBSERVER AGREEMENT

To help both teachers and behavioral scientists working in education draw the conclusions necessary for making daily decisions and solving problems, there must be agreement on the observational bases for these conclusions or inferences. Agreement among observers relates to the adequacy with which behaviors are defined and the complexity of behavior and characteristics of the setting (Bramlett & Barnett, 1993). Precise, unambiguous specifications of what behavioral activities are to be focused on are prerequisite to structuring or organizing behavioral observations. Such precision in defining an observed behavior increases the extent to which various observers report similarly about the behavior on which they have focused. The goal is for two observers of the same situation to focus on the same child behaviors and agree about what they see or hear.

The greater the agreement between two independent observers, the greater the consistency or "reliability" of both viewers. For example, if teacher A and teacher B are both observing Jimmy, a 7-year-old second-grader, during reading group, their observations are likely to differ if they do not share a *clear definition* of what behaviors they should focus on. They are not likely to draw a consistent conclusion about Jimmy's attention to reading materials if they have not focused on the same attentive behaviors at the same point in time.

Furthermore, precise definitions force individual observers to be consistent with themselves. The more precise the definition, the less the opportunity for subjectivity to be introduced into the observation process. (More detailed discussions of the various types of reliability can be found in Everston & Green, 1986; Foster & Cone, 1986; Hartmann, 1982; Hollenbeck, 1978; Kent & Foster, 1977; Page & Iwata, 1986.) For example, if teacher A wants to count the number of times preschoolers in a defined setting display "dependency" behavior, the teacher will have difficulty consistently labeling specific behaviors "dependent" unless he or she has made a careful listing of dependent behaviors before observing. Generally, the more specific and complete these criteria for labeling behaviors, the more consistent the observer will be in pinpointing behaviors over time with himself or herself or other observers (see Figure 7.1).

Many readers of the educational and behavioral science literature will discover reports on the *inter-rater reliability* for a particular observation instrument. These statements of agreement among observers in recording observations are generally indicated in the form of reliability coefficients, which range from the point of no agreement (0) to perfect observer agreement (+1.0). Generally, one tends to find reliability coefficients reported in the range of +.70 to +.95. As the coefficient approaches +1.0, the reliability increases, and we have more confidence in reliable observations among observers.

The rate of agreement between two or more observers working at the same time can be determined as shown in Figure 7.2. Observers

FIGURE 7.1. Observer Agreement

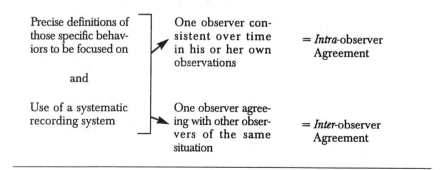

FIGURE 7.2. **Determining Rate of Agreement Between Observers**

Example: Teacher questioning patterns in a seventh-grade social studies class

Steps	Category	Observer A	Observer B
1. Count the number of instances in each category for observers A and B.	Teacher asks for: Specific fact Opinion Application	~~////~~ // //// /	~~////~~ /// //
2. Total the number of observations for A and B.	Total	12 + 10 = 22	
3. Count the number of agreements in each category and over categories for both observers.	Agreements: Specific fact Opinion Application Total		5 3 + 1 9
4. Divide the number of agreements by the total number of observations.		9/22 = .409	
5. Multiply the quotient by the number of observers; in this example there are two.	2 x .409 = .82 Rate of Agreement = .82		

should aim for rates of agreement of .80 or better. Note that we have no check using this procedure as to whether the same behavior instances were observed, but only the rate of agreement between observers. If, however, we employed a time-sampling system (see Unit VIII), by which each observer records only one behavior during each observational interval (that is, every 5 seconds), we could also determine whether the same behaviors were being observed.

Once an observer has determined his or her rate of agreement with another observer, the decision may be made to follow the same procedures without the second observer being present. It is useful, however, for observers periodically to spot-check their rates of agreement in order to assure accuracy.

Another procedure for assessing observer agreement is in fact to consider instances where *behavior does not occur* (Hartmann, 1982; Page & Iwata, 1986; Vasta, 1979). In the same situation, two observers can:

- Agree that a behavior occurred
- Disagree, in that observer 1 indicates a behavior occurred, while observer 2 does not
- Disagree, in that observer 2 indicates a behavior occurred, while observer 1 does not
- Agree that a behavior did not occur

Thus, one can evaluate the rate of agreement for occurring and non-occurring behavior or events. Baker and Tyne (1980) have suggested that the use of the formula for observer agreement described in Figure 7.2 can overestimate agreement when behaviors or events occur with high frequency. In contrast, observation of infrequent behaviors or events can result in lower reliabilities. In such cases, one might also consider intervals when only one observer notes the behavior or when both agree that behaviors did not occur.

STABILITY OF OBSERVATIONS ACROSS TIME

Observer agreement, although essential, is insufficient to assess the reliability of one's observational system. Repeated visits must be made to a setting over a brief span of time (1 to 2 weeks) in order to establish the stability of observations. For example, if one were concerned about a group of students completing their math assignments, it would be necessary to observe these students over time to determine if a consistent pattern of behavior was exhibited. If "aggressive" behavior was exhibited by two pupils, the teacher might question if this was a chance occurrence. The teacher would have to observe the pupils over time. By correlating the observational outcomes for two or more occasions, a *stability coefficient* can be obtained. (For detailed descriptions of calculating stability measures, see Foster & Cone, 1986; Kent & Foster, 1977; and Rowley, 1976, 1978.)

In establishing the stability of observations, one raises the practical question of how many observations are required in order to have confidence in the findings. Clearly, there is no one correct answer for this question—the number of observations needed and the schedule for observing are tied to the observer's purpose.

Consider these different observation questions and the frequency of observations required in order to produce stable, reliable observation outcomes.

1. How do the spatial concepts "top" and "bottom" develop in preschool 3- and 4-year-old children?
   - Repeat observations of the same children over time; for example, once per month for a year.
   - Alternatively, observe a number of children at different age levels performing the same tasks.
2. What pattern of peer interactions does Jesse display?
   - Observe Jesse a minimum of three times in situations where peer interaction is possible.
3. Does a behavioral intervention improve Mary's on-task behavior in mathematics?
   - Observe Mary during mathematics for 5 minutes each day for 1 week prior to the intervention (baseline).
   - Next, observe Mary for 5 minutes each day in mathematics during the intervention.
   - After an appropriate time period, try removing the intervention and record Mary's behavior daily.
   - Return to the intervention, if necessary, to maintain improved behavior and continue to collect observational data daily.

When conducting psychoeducational research using observational techniques, one will often demand a greater number of observations in order to draw conclusions than when arriving at daily decisions in the classroom. In the research context, one will probably observe in a range of different situations, classrooms, or schools before confidently generalizing about the effects of an intervention, the impact of a teaching strategy, or the value of a curricular innovation.

Rowley (1978) has reviewed some interesting work by John Herbert and associates at the Ontario Institute for Studies in Education that helps set guidelines for collecting observational data. Each of 30 teachers was observed for 50 minutes on six to seven occasions, using the "System for Analyzing Lessons." Rowley focused on how the reliability of observational data is affected by (1) the number of observation periods, (2) the length of the observation period, and (3) the combination of varying the number and length of observation periods. Three major conclusions were drawn:

1. Reliability increased with more frequent observation periods.
2. Although reliability increased with the length of the observa-

tion period, the greatest increment occurred when the observation period was increased from 10 to 20 minutes. After 20 minutes, the reliability leveled off.

3. The optimal combination of number and length of observation periods was five periods of 30 minutes each ($r = .705$).

However, the implication of this work for the classroom observer with limited time and resources is to make three observations of 30 minutes duration or to arrange four observational periods of 20 minutes duration. The length of these observational periods could be accommodated by typical class schedules.

The use of repeated observations, whether using an observation schedule, a checklist, or a rating scale, is particularly important with preschoolers, who are notably inconsistent as their skills are emerging. The goal is to obtain a sufficient sample of behavior in order to gain a consistent picture of a child's functioning.

CHALLENGES TO RELIABLE OBSERVATIONS

Unfortunately, gathering reliable observational data is not an automatic, commonsense, "anyone can do it" activity. There are many sources of error that can creep into the process, distorting the validity of the conclusions based on the data. An extensive literature documents different sources of error or bias (e.g., Baker & Tyne, 1980; Evertson & Green, 1986; Fassnacht, 1982; Kazdin, 1982; Kent & Foster, 1977; Page & Iwata, 1986; Taplin & Reid, 1973). Error can derive from the *observer*, the *observee*, and the *observation system*. Each of these potential sources of bias will be highlighted, and possible solutions to the problems suggested.

Observer Bias

Perhaps the most significant sources of error are observers themselves.

Personal Bias or Expectation. Let's consider an example involving Janie, a pleasant and cooperative 6-year-old. She completes her assignments on time, and the teacher likes her and expects her to do well. A new girl joins the class and is being teased by some of the other girls. The teacher, wanting to get at the source of the problem, observes and records "teasing" behavior in the classroom. Although Janie makes faces at the newcomer, the teacher overlooks this behavior. Bias has occurred due to the teacher's beliefs and expectations about Janie. As explained earlier, when such bias is positive, placing the observee in a favorable light, it is called a "halo effect"; when the bias is negative, it might be called "prejudice." Thus, prior experiences between the observer and observee can influence the outcomes of observation (Kazdin, 1982).

Systematic training can help the observer increase objectivity by facilitating awareness of one's personal beliefs and biases. Since each of us has different tolerance levels or thresholds for different situations, we need to be attuned to our attitudes about such distracting behaviors as an individual's "good" manners, quick response styles, or repetitive question-asking. A "violent outburst" of anger to one observer might be seen as "within normal limits" by another (Good & Brophy, 1991).

Potential biases associated with an observer's sex, race, age, and cultural or ethnic identity must all be addressed in the particular observational setting. Finally, the theoretical perspective of the viewer (developmental, behavioral, humanistic, or whatever) can certainly affect or color what one sees and how it is perceived.

One needs to have an accurate perception of potential sources of personal bias.

Knowledge of Hypotheses. In pursuing observational research, it has been widely demonstrated that observers who know the purpose of the study or the hypotheses being tested will more likely record observations that tend to support the hypotheses. Therefore, to correct such potential biases, most research designs include observers who are "blind" to the purposes of the study.

In classroom life, such controls are not always feasible. However, a colleague of the observer (another teacher, an educational specialist, a school psychologist, or another professional) might observe in a targeted classroom, unaware of the specific problem or the particular child who is experiencing a problem (Baker & Tyne, 1980).

Observer Drift. Observers often use instruments or procedures that require extensive pretraining to achieve observer agreement. Once in the field, after having employed the instrument for a length of time, the observer will frequently begin to "drift" when recording observations, becoming less precise and less accurate. Drift of another type might occur: Observers who always work together will tend to agree ("consensual drift"); their observations will become more alike over time (Hartmann, 1982). When possible, the use of regular, unannounced reliability spot-checks to monitor an observer's accuracy is warranted. This might be accomplished by having two observers in the setting during a selected sample of sessions. When a large number of observations are gathered, approximately 10–20% of the total should be checked; with a small number of observations, a minimum of two checks should be made.

Inadequate Training. The most inexcusable source of observer error is poor training. Many observation systems must be practiced extensively before being used in a classroom setting. Adequate time must be allowed for practicing, feedback, and guided discussion. The practice might take many forms, such as use of videotapes or team observing. A criterion level of 90% agreement with an expert observer's ratings should be achieved prior to employing an observation instrument. When actually using an observation system in the field, agreement of at least 80% is desirable and depends on the decision to be made (Barnett & MacMann, 1992; Bramlett & Barnett, 1993). Observers need to know and practice the rules and procedures of any observational system they use. See Boice (1983) for detailed suggestions on improving observational skills.

Some suggestions for training activities include

Memorizing the code with quizzes to check knowledge
Watching a video and recording observations using the code
Discussing disagreements
Checking observations against a completed protocol
Observing in the field with a co-observer

Bias Related to the Observee

Changes in the Observee. The teacher observing in his or her own classroom is known to the pupils and is expected to be observing them. Consequently, students are not as likely to alter their behavior in the teacher's presence. (Certainly, if a forbidden activity is being pursued and the teacher approaches the scene, children will change their behavior quickly!)

Individuals also modify some of their behavior when an outside observer enters the setting and when they know they are being observed. This change in behavior is generally referred to as "reactivity."

Knowledge of Being Observed. If individuals know they are being observed, and particularly if they know why, they might behave in ways to please the observer, such as remaining in their seats, raising their hands more often, or asking more questions. Other individuals become more nervous and display signs of anxiety not normally shown.

Ethics, of course, dictates that individuals who do not belong in a particular setting must receive permission (from observees or their parents) to observe in classrooms, testing rooms, or other settings. It is not easy to hide the fact of being observed from even the youngest child.

Despite these obstacles, steps might be taken to reduce observee reactivity:

1. The observer can visit the classroom or other setting several times, so that students become accustomed to his or her presence. Usually one or two visits is sufficient for younger children. Older children might have more visits to become acclimated; early observations may have to be discarded.
2. Participant observers such as other teachers, paraprofessionals, and older students might be employed and be less obtrusive than strangers (Baker & Tyne, 1980).
3. Observation rooms with one-way mirrors might alleviate reactivity more quickly, but in most cases one cannot observe classroom settings this way. Also, if observees turn their backs to a one-way mirror, many behaviors are not seen.

Intrusiveness of Equipment. The use of video recordings or tape recordings (see Unit X for more detailed discussion), although solving some of the problems that arise from an observer's presence, can be intrusive. The equipment must be introduced to the setting, not unlike introducing a human observer. Small, hand-held camcorders now available to teachers reduce this problem.

When we videotaped preschool classrooms, for example, we set up the equipment a day ahead of time and used the opportunity for trial runs. The children soon adapted to the cameras, cables, and equipment operators. The activities of the day quickly became more interesting than the video intruders. The one significant distractor was a microphone that reminded some children of a gun; a quick modification was made.

The Observation System as a Source of Errors

Two issues must be considered to minimize possible errors due to the observation system: the match of the system and the complexity of the observational procedure.

Match of the System. When observers in classrooms select from available observation instruments, they must consider if an instrument effectively matches their observational purposes. Are the behaviors targeted by the selected instrument appropriate and sufficiently detailed to address the questions raised by the observer? The issue is paramount as well when observers develop their own instrument. This match relates to the validity of the observational measure, a topic discussed in Unit VIII.

Complexity of the Observational Procedures. The more complex an observational system, the greater the opportunity for error. Systems that require many decisions on the part of the observer, involve complex categories, or demand memorization of many codes are more vulnerable to error. The use of clear, precise observational questions and simple, non-overlapping coding categories reduces the possibility of such error.

Our discussion of the sources of observational error has highlighted some of the threats to reliable observational data. Accounting for reliability is essential if one is to have confidence in observational techniques. A brief checklist, presented in Figure 7.3, summarizes the critical issues discussed in this unit.

FIGURE 7.3. **Summary Checklist for Making Reliable Observations**

Issue	Considerations
1. Objectivity	Specific behaviors listed beforehand
	Eliminating bias due to personal belief or expectation
	Awareness of developmental expectations across the cultural/language groups served
	Not knowing the hypotheses
2. Clear, usable recording format	Nonoverlapping categories
	Avoiding complex coding systems
3. Inter-observer agreement	Aiming for 80% or better
	Adequate training
4. Avoiding observer drift	Systematic spot-checks
	Two observers present 10–20% of time

Sampling and Recording Behavior, Considering Validity, and Using Observational Outcomes

Once an observer has selected appropriate categories of behavior on which to focus (Unit VI) and in order to maximize reliable observing (Unit VII), it is necessary to devise a plan for systematically sampling observations in the setting. The approach is the same as that of the microbiologist who wants to determine the purity of water in a lake for drinking purposes but who, for obvious reasons, cannot test the whole lake. This scientist draws test samples from many parts of the lake so that the total sample will be representative of the lake as a whole. Moreover, samples are drawn at different times, so that they will be representative over an extended period of time. Such sampling is also required in classroom observation.

SAMPLING PROCEDURES

One issue facing the observer confronting the myriad behaviors that occur over time is the procedure for selecting specific behaviors for observation. For example, the observer may opt to record all behaviors of a given child during the school day (generally referred to as a diary description or running record). However, while one is observing this one child, the behaviors of the other children, perhaps engaged in similar activities, will be missed. Therefore, it is vital for the observer to decide ahead of time on the sampling procedures to be employed. Two useful sampling procedures, *time sampling* and *event sampling*, have been detailed by Wright (1960) and are described in the next two sections. Each can be used to quantify information and to track a child's progress, teacher's activity, or the effectiveness of an intervention.

Time Sampling

According to Wright (1960), the observer using a time sampling procedure attends to the occurrence or nonoccurrence of selected behavior(s) (signs, events) within specified, uniform time limits. "The length, spacing, and number of intervals are intended to secure representative time samples of the target phenomena. As a rule . . . descriptive categories are coded in advance for quick and precise judgements in the field and later efficient scoring" (p. 93). Thus, the length, spacing, and number of time units are determined by the purpose of the observer. Time sampling is an appropriate procedure to sample behaviors that occur in rapid succession, such as children's interactions or teacher verbalizations.

An example of time sampling would be the case of an observer interested in the ability of second-grade students to remain on a specified learning task. He could check each of 25 students for 10 seconds every 5 minutes, throughout a given part of the science period, to see whether each was "off-task" or not. A descriptive list of behaviors to be considered off-task would have been made prior to the observation, and it would include such particulars as "looking around the room," "being out of seat," and "engaged in unrelated activities." For another observer question, the appropriate sample interval might be every minute, or every 10 minutes, or every day of a week, or during other subject time periods.

Developing a Sampling Schedule

Sampling of children's behavior using time units can be done in a number of ways. The observer can

- Use a check to indicate whether a behavior occurred in the time interval, such as a child's using a particular language form
- Tally the number of times a behavior occurs during the time unit, such as hand raising
- Indicate whether a behavior lasted the whole unit, such as a child staying on task

The observer can also tell whether the behavior of interest occurred at all during the time unit.

One suitable worksheet format is given in Figure 8.1, Procedure A. Here, each child's off-task behavior would be recorded at each sample interval, using as many lines as necessary for the number of children being observed. Again note that a list of off-task behaviors would have to be drawn up ahead of time.

It is important to use a simple form of coding or abbreviating that facilitates recording of the observed behaviors. In Procedure A, where

FIGURE 8.1. Time Sampling

Procedure A: "Off-task" Behavior*

Time Unit

Child	10:00	10:05	10:10	10:15	10:20	10:25	10:30	Total

* Within each time unit observe each child for 10 seconds, record for 10 seconds, move on to the next child, and so forth. Tally each occurrence of "off-task" behavior.

Procedure B: "Off-task" Behavior (Pre-coded)

Child	10:00			10:05			10:10			10:15			10:20			10:25			10:30			Total		
	L	O	U	L	O	U	L	O	U	L	O	U	L	O	U	L	O	U	L	O	U	L	O	U

only one category is involved, no coding is required; a checkmark for any 10-second interval records an occurrence of off-task behavior. Using longer time intervals for each child, the observer might use tallies to record several discrete occurrences of a behavior in each interval.

Another observer, however, concerned with subcategories of off-task behavior, would develop a coding system for the specific behaviors. This is shown in Figure 8.1, Procedure B. In this example, the observer has determined this code:

L = Looking around (seated)
O = Out of seat
U = Unrelated activity (seated)

Off-task behavior would be indicated by a checkmark in the L, O, or U column; no mark would indicate on-task behavior. The observer would use as many lines as necessary for the number of children being observed.

It should be noted that exactly the same information recorded on the Procedure B worksheet could have been recorded on the uncoded Procedure A worksheet. Instead of simply making a checkmark for a given 10-second unit, the observer using Procedure A could write L, O, or U, depending on which category of off-task behavior was observed. However, an advantage of having the categories precoded on the recording form is that it is much easier to make checkmarks under coded columns than to memorize and record the code. Another advantage is that when sampling is completed, the results are already tabulated. The observer can easily calculate the frequency with which each child exhibits each form of off-task behavior and establish intervention plans.

The coding system (the categories and their codes) must always, of course, be memorized before sampling begins; moreover, the observer should always have an outline of the coding system at hand in case of memory lapses. Obviously a system can be most easily and reliably memorized if the codes are abbreviated or other symbols are designed to remind the observer of the categories themselves. (As codes for the off-task behaviors categorized above, the letter abbreviations L, O, and U are easier to remember than the numbers 1, 2, and 3 would be.) And when such codes are present as tabulators on the record form, they constantly reinforce the observer's memory of the coding system.

Such helps are extremely valuable in time sampling. Remember that the observer must proceed from one preset time interval to the next, ready or not. The difficulty of using a memorized coding system is of course greatest when the time units are very short (the Flanders system requires the observer to record a code number every 3 seconds) and the number of categories is relatively large. The procedure can be taxing, and its efficient use requires considerable practice.

The more detailed the coding system used, the fewer the number of individuals that can be observed in a given time interval. Before observing, one has to create a balance between

The most appropriate time unit
The number of individuals to be observed
The detail desired from the observation

In general, observers should

1. Determine the appropriate time interval that will allow them to sample key behaviors
2. Facilitate recording through using a simple code and format
3. Allow for recording time (when the observer is not also trying to observe)

Going back to the example of on-task behavior in a second-grade class cited earlier, the observer could decide to observe only a sample of the 25 pupils present and obtain even more frequent or detailed observational data on each child.

Generally, time sampling is useful for observing behaviors that occur frequently and at a somewhat regular rate. Observers, however, have to be aware that time sampling can overestimate low frequency or brief behaviors (Mann, Ten Have, Plunkett, & Meisels, 1991). Wolery (1989) suggests that time sampling should be based on a minimum of 20 opportunities to respond.

Event Sampling

Event sampling simply allows the observer to record a given event or category of events each time it naturally occurs. When the event occurs, the observer codes it using a coding system, or describes it and, if desired, describes the antecedents to and/or the consequences of that event. The range of events one might choose to record is practically limitless and, again depending on one's purpose, might range from pupils' use of language to demonstrations of independent study skills. However, as Shapiro and Skinner (1990) point out, event sampling is most effective when used with behaviors that have a defined beginning and end, with low to moderate rates of occurrence, and last for short periods of time. The major advantage of event sampling is that it allows one to observe events as they naturally occur and in context. For example, a preschool or special education teacher might be interested in pupils' self-help skills, determining ahead of time to observe such skills as

Going to the bathroom unassisted
Washing hands
Buttoning clothing
Putting on boots
Tying shoelaces

The teacher may observe and record for each child the date on which that child acquired these skills or when these events occurred. This form of sampling is reflected in many checklists the teacher might develop for use in the classroom. A recording format such as the one presented in Figure 8.2 might be employed for these observations. The observer would use as many columns as necessary for the behaviors being observed and as many lines as necessary for the number of children, and would record the date on which the child demonstrates the skill.

While maintaining a record such as this, the teacher can determine the frequency of the behavior for a specific child or group of children. (In a class with children presenting special needs, the categories might have to be broken down into finer units.)

An important outcome of time and event sampling is that two observers can simultaneously view and record the same events, permitting later determination of the extent of observer agreement or consistency in sampling and recording observations. This information can then be used to document when the child has attained desired learning or behavioral objectives such as "Is able to use the bathroom unassisted in a consistent manner (at least 5 consecutive days)."

Time Versus Event Sampling

In summary, time and event sampling have distinct advantages and limitations, which are presented in Figure 8.3.

Many systems combine time and event sampling. For example, the frequency and nature of events such as teacher praise are of interest to many educators. The *Teacher Approval/Disapproval Classroom Record*

FIGURE 8.2. **Event Sampling Procedures**

Self-help Skills

Child	Bathroom Unassisted	Washes Hands	Buttons Clothes	Puts on Boots	Ties Shoelaces

FIGURE 8.3. Time versus Event Sampling

Advantages	Limitations
TIME SAMPLING	

Advantages	Limitations
• Good agreement among observers.	• Infrequent events may not be represented accurately.
• Good reliability over time.	• The duration of events is not assessed.
• Good control over the mechanics of the system.	• The frequency with which the events of interest occur may not be represented accurately—e.g., events that occur frequently within a time unit may be underrepresented in total calculations if a +/- system per time unit is used.
• Good overview of the range of behaviors and events occurring in a particular setting.	

EVENT SAMPLING

Advantages	Limitations
• Helpful in describing events of a particular kind that have been detailed before the observation takes place.	• Breaks up the natural continuity of behavior.
• Every natural occurrence of targeted behavior is sampled.	• May not provide information as to what set off a particular event.

(*TAD*) (White, Beecher, et al., 1973) views the rate of teacher verbal approvals (A) and disapprovals (D) during daily instruction. Taking into account when a class period starts and finishes, the observer notes the time at which each approving or disapproving teacher behavior occurs. The specific pupil behavior and teacher responses are recorded, along with pupil characteristics (Figure 8.4).

This system is interesting in that a recording interval of 20 seconds is employed whenever an approval or disapproval occurs. The total amount of recording time (the number of such intervals multiplied by 20 seconds) is subtracted from the total observation time, allowing the rate of actual observation to be calculated. (However, as with other systems, another approval or disapproval could occur during the recording time and not be included.) The results of 16 studies (in K–12) employing *TAD* (White, 1975) have shown that:

1. Teacher approvals are highest in grades 1 and 2, after which they decline sharply, to four to eight approvals during a class period.
2. Teacher disapprovals also decline after the primary grades.
3. Teacher approvals occur more frequently than disapprovals in grades 1 and 2, but thereafter disapprovals occur more frequently than approvals.
4. Teacher approval rate is higher for ongoing instruction than for classroom management.
5. Teachers emit more approvals to pupils learning at a faster rate than to those working at a slower rate.

Thus, the usefulness of this time and event measure has been well documented.

Interval Recording and Accounting for Duration

In addition to time and event sampling, procedures are available to help observers evaluate behavior in ongoing situations. These include interval recording and accounting for duration.

Interval recording involves dividing the observation period into time intervals. Thus, a 30-minute class period might be divided into 10 intervals of 3 minutes each. Depending on the observation purpose and system, the observer using interval recording can detail:

- The occurrence and nonoccurrence of behaviors
- The frequency of target behaviors within each interval
- The duration of behavior within an interval
- The portion (beginning, middle, end) of the interval in which the behavior occurred

FIGURE 8.4. Sample *TAD* Recording (A= APPROVAL; D= DISAPPROVAL)

Time Start	Activity	Time	Teacher Response	Pupil Behavior
9:17 A.M.	Reading group, 5 boys	1 hr. 45 min.	1. You're not telling me what it means. (D)	Incorrect answer to question.
End of class period, 11:02 A.M.			2. Right (A)	Correct answer to question.

When observers are interested in how long a child's behavior is maintained (such as how long a disruptive behavior lasts or how long a highly distractable child can stay seated), they engage in what is referred to as duration recording using a timing device. Recording duration allows observers to report not only the frequency of behaviors but also the persistence of behavior over time. Thus, a teacher could observe exactly how long a child persisted with an activity or how much time a child was off-task during an instructional period. If brief time intervals are involved, a timing device will be needed. (For more details see Alessi & Kaye, 1983; Foster & Cone, 1986; Shapiro, 1987; Shapiro & Skinner, 1990.) This kind of information is important to document progress before and after a teacher begins an intervention program.

Other Aspects of Sampling

Number of Behavior Categories Used. The number of behaviors an observer can take account of at one point in time is limited. According to Medley and Mitzel (1963),

> The number of categories into which the behaviors are to be coded should not be too large; few studies have used more than ten. It seems desirable to define the categories so that their average frequencies are roughly equal, but experience has shown that in some instances categories used less than 5% of the time function effectively. (p. 330)

Use of more than 10 or 12 categories, however, makes serious demands on memory and requires extensive training. This issue is particularly challenging for early childhood observers and special educators who might be interested in such issues as the articulation of speech sounds or the accuracy of gross-motor movements.

Representativeness of the Behavior Sample. In order to determine the representativeness of most behaviors, it is necessary to observe the occurrence of a given behavior at different times of the day, across activities, and on different occasions. If a behavior happens only once or on rare occasions, it is not representative of overall behavior. Therefore, before making conclusions, it is important to assess the *frequency* of the behaviors.

Anecdotal records are a case in point. Records are often made of unusual behaviors ("He stole the money that was on my desk.") or of only one form of behavior (more likely to be negative than positive). Unfortunately, such information frequently follows an individual, even if it is not representative of that individual's overall functioning. In the final analysis, anecdotal information cannot be given much weight unless a record of the frequency of the behavior in question has been kept, as well as its frequency relative to other behaviors for that individual and a broader sample of individuals. Within the classroom, then, we may decide to observe a number of times during different periods of the day, as well as on different days of the week, and within the different behavioral settings—classroom, gym, playground, and so on. Task 11 will test your ability to take a representative sample.

TASK 11: DETERMINING REPRESENTATIVE OBSERVATIONAL SAMPLES

Indicate which of the samples given on the Task 11 Worksheet are likely to yield representative observations. Check your responses with the sample responses given in the Appendix.

Who Is Sampled? In addition to systematic sampling of behaviors, it is frequently necessary to sample pupils. For example, if our purpose were to determine whether kindergarten pupils in a particular school system encountered difficulty with letter recognition, we would not need to observe every child. Rather, we might want to select for study a random, unbiased sample of 10 pupils (for example, every third pupil according to last name in alphabetical order; or we could write the children's names on slips of paper, place them in a hat, and draw out our random sample of 10 pupils) from each of the kindergarten classrooms in the school system. On the other hand, for diagnostic purposes, an individual teacher may wish to observe every pupil's skills.

Another observer, interested in observing first-grade pupils' spontaneous use of relational terms such as "more" and "less," may, in a representative first-grade classroom, observe five pupils for 10 minutes and so on until all pupils have been observed. This cycle can be repeated several times.

A useful sampling system reported in Kowatrakul (1959), which is referred to as *point-sampling*, allows the observer to view a pupil long enough to record one of a given series of behaviors, then move on to the next pupil until a given behavior occurs, and so on. Kowatrakul used this technique to study the relation between pupil behavior and classroom activities in various subject areas.

Another useful procedure suggested by Alessi and Kaye (1983) when observing a child whose behavior is of concern is to randomly select and observe another child whose behavior is considered typical. A com-

Task 11 Worksheet

Determining Representative Observational Samples

Problem or Question	Behavior Sample	Representative?		Reasons for Your Response
		Yes	No	
Study of first-grade children's "on task" behavior in school.	Observe the behavior of children sitting in a front-row seat of each row in a particular class.			
Count of out-of-seat behaviors of an "acting-out" kindergartner.	Observe the child on 5 successive days from 10:00 A.M. to 10:15 A.M.			
Study the extent to which 5-year-old children interact in same-sex, opposite-sex, or mixed-sex groupings on the playground.	Randomly choose four boys and four girls. Observe each child's behavior on a systematic rotation basis for 5 minutes, indicating the amount of time each child interacts in designated categories. Sampling should be done on different days and at different times.			

parison of observations between these two pupils can help the observer understand if the first child's behavior is considerably different, how the behaviors differ, and patterns of teacher interaction with the two pupils.

RECORDING OBSERVATIONAL DATA

An essential component of the observation process is the immediate recording of the behaviors observed. As noted in our discussion of time and event sampling, the observer cannot depend on memory; rather, the observer must use a recording sheet, if reliable data are to be collected. This recording sheet must be designed so that the information can be easily summarized. Although a broad variety of recording sheets can be found in the literature, the "Flanders Interaction Analysis Categories" (discussed in Simon & Boyer, 1969), developed over 25 years ago, is a category system for collecting teacher–pupil interactions that involves the use of simple recording procedures.

The Flanders system has been one of the most widely used observation schemes and has been taught to teachers, student teachers, supervisors, and counselors who want to view and understand their typical patterns of verbal exchange with students in the classroom. Flanders offers 10 categories for classifying verbal behaviors, which are shown in Figure 8.5. Flanders simply numbers the 10 categories sequentially from 1 to 10. After memorizing the code, the observer need only write down a single number to represent a type of verbal activity. The observer can write a stream of numbers that represent what is occurring in the classroom. As Simon and Boyer (1969) have noted, the observer "will have no record of what has been said but he will have a record which allows him to infer the classroom climate and describe the teaching style" (p. 116). In recording observations, the observer makes a notation for every change in category and also records one category number at least every 3 seconds whether there is a category change or not. (See Flanders, 1970, for a discussion of a 22-category system, which is a more extensive subdivision of the basic 10 categories.)

A data sheet for 1 minute of consecutive observation and sequential coding of teacher–pupil verbal behaviors using the Flanders system would look like the sample record shown in Figure 8.6. By reading down the columns of numbers collected by the observer, one gets a picture of the sequence of verbal behaviors that occurred during the 1-minute time period. After collecting these "raw" observational data over a more representative time sample than 1 minute, the observer can transcribe the

FIGURE 8.5. **Flanders Categories for Classifying Behavior**

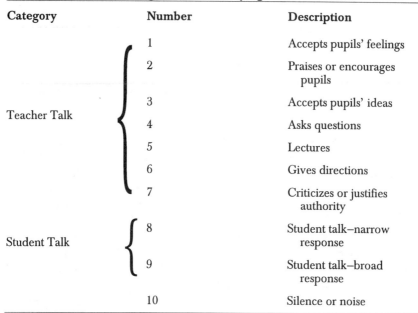

Category	Number	Description
Teacher Talk	1	Accepts pupils' feelings
	2	Praises or encourages pupils
	3	Accepts pupils' ideas
	4	Asks questions
	5	Lectures
	6	Gives directions
	7	Criticizes or justifies authority
Student Talk	8	Student talk–narrow response
	9	Student talk–broad response
	10	Silence or noise

Source: Simon & Boyer (1969), p. 118–119

data to a summary grid that provides a "picture" of the frequency of various kinds of teacher and pupil verbal activity occurring in the classroom setting. (It is generally recommended that a 20-minute observation [400 tallies] be used as a reasonable minimum for generating a picture of the verbal activity in a classroom. Simon & Boyer [1969] offer an excellent detailed description of the procedures for transcribing Flanders categories to a summary matrix.)

The observer can easily compute the percentage of time during the observation period that a particular kind of verbal behavior occurred. Also, by summarizing the observational data, the pattern or strategies used by a teacher in the classroom can be revealed. Questions such as the following can be answered with the Flanders system:

How often do pupils talk in the classroom?
How much do pupils talk in comparison with their teacher?
Do pupils talk to each other or only to the teacher?
How does the teacher reinforce different kinds of student behavior?

What strategies does the teacher employ to involve students in classroom discussion?

By using the Flanders approach with these questions, the observer can begin to draw conclusions about classroom climate and make inferences about the communication strategies fostered in the classroom. Extensive information can be generated from a simple, sequential recording of category numbers on the page. The Flanders approach has been the forerunner of a wide range of observational techniques for the study of teaching and learning processes in educational settings (Evertson & Green, 1986). We have presented the Flanders system because of its simplicity and usefulness.

A number of observation systems have been developed for use with young children. One example, the "Preschool Observation Code" (POC; Bramlett & Barnett, 1993), is a new system developed for young children with an intervention base in the research literature. The POC is a category system that was developed to be used by practitioners to analyze frequent problem behaviors, such as attending problems, throughout the assessment-intervention process. This code takes into account both the behavior of the child and setting characteristics that might be important for intervention. The POC focuses on three broad classes of problem behaviors (conduct problems, social withdrawal or isolation, and attending behavior related to learning problems). Classroom conditions include large-group instruction, small-group instruction, free play, and individual work. The POC includes 9 categories of behavior of some duration (states), such as play engagement and social interaction, and 11 event categories, such as activity changes and teacher interaction. It employs both time sampling and frequency recording for

FIGURE 8.6. **Verbal Behavior Data Sheet**

Setting: Mrs. Jones first-grade class **Activity:** Current events discussion			**Date:** June 3 **Time:** 10:50 to 10:51 A.M.	
(1) 4	(5) 5	(9) 7	(13) 5	(17) 7
(2) 9	(6) 6	(10) 7	(14) 9	(18) 7
(3) 9	(7) 9	(11) 6	(15) 9	(19) 4
(4) 4	(8) 7	(12) 5	(16) 9	(20) 4

(Digits following numbers in parentheses indicate code.)

events. A tape provides prompts every 30 seconds for 20 intervals (10 minutes of observation). The observer first looks at the child and scores the state category and then uses the remainder of the interval to record event behaviors. Procedures for training observers and technical data are detailed.

Another example is the *Ecobehavioral System for Complex Assessment of the Preschool Environment* (*ESCAPE*; Carta, Greenwood, & Atwater, 1985). *ESCAPE* is an example of an important preschool coding system that consists of 101 codes in 12 categories, six covering the ecology of the classroom (such as task materials and activity structure), three covering teacher behaviors, and three covering student behaviors. This system is used in research programs to assess the effectiveness of intervention received by a target child and provides observers with detailed information about the interactions between the teacher and the child, taking into account characteristics of instruction and the setting. *ESCAPE* was designed to provide detailed information about the classroom program received by a target student and involves a complex code that requires considerable training. Procedures for training observers and technical data are provided.

OTHER RECORDING FORMATS

In this section, two additional sample recording formats are suggested. Both formats can be easily adapted by the teacher/observer to suit his or her own particular observation goal.

With Sample Worksheet A (see Figure 8.7), the observer can

Detail the units or categories of behavior that constitute a particular area of concern (columns)
List the children to be observed (rows)
Tally the frequency of observed behaviors for each child within a given observation period (total across each row)
Tally the frequency of each behavior for all of the children observed (total down each column)
Total all observed behaviors (total rows × total columns)

In using this worksheet, the observer would list the categories of behavior to be observed in the diagonal columns across the top of the form.

The format given on Sample Worksheet A can be used with both category and sign systems, and is easily adaptable to recording observations over time. If one were to use different colored pencils in tally-

FIGURE 8.7. Sample Worksheet A

								Total A	Comment
Child									
Total B									**Grand Total**

Total A is total of all observed behaviors demonstrated by a particular child.
Total B is total for each unit of behavior observed for all of the children combined.
Grand Total is total of all observed behaviors.

ing behaviors at different times, one could quickly "eyeball" differences among children and by the same child at different times.

By using the format of Worksheet A, we have recorded some observations about the language used by two students during free play (see Figure 8.8). Verbally transcribing the observations, we learn that during the observation period Jill never used complete sentences but used relational terms; Jack used complete sentences, but did not use relational terms. We also learn that both Jill and Jack asked questions but that Jack asked more questions.

Sample Worksheet B (Figure 8.9) provides a format an observer could use to note the variety of behaviors engaged in by one child or by a group of children throughout the course of a school day. The specific behaviors or particular activities that are to be observed would be listed in the diagonal columns at the center of the worksheet. This section could, of course, be extended to include as many activities or behaviors as the observer wanted to note. The "Observation Begins" and "Observation

FIGURE 8.8. **Language Use During Free Play**

Date: _____   Time: _____   to _____

Behaviors of Interest

Child	Uses Complete Sentences	Asks Questions for Information	Uses Relational Concepts	Total A	Comment
Jack Jones	IIII	‖‖ I	0		
Jill Brown	0	III	II		
Total B					Grand Total

Ends" columns enable the observer to continue using one worksheet while major shifts in classroom activity occur.

As an example of how to use Sample Worksheet B, consider the steps a teacher would take when observing patterns of cooperative behavior in a classroom:

1. Define the variety of behaviors that indicate cooperation.
2. List these categories of behavior (or activities) in the diagonal columns across the top of the worksheet.
3. When beginning to observe, indicate the time.
4. Note the activity period in progress.
5. Tally the occurrence of each category of activity that occurs in the appropriate column.
6. Note the time each observation period ends.

Alternatively, the teacher could use the same format over time and record the date a child demonstrates cooperative behavior (and details of the situation, if desired). The observer would repeat the entire process using a sufficient number of observation periods to adequately answer the question posed.

Worksheet A and Worksheet B provide samples of the types of simple instruments that can be devised for recording and organizing observational information. Planning systematic recording procedures ahead of time both facilitates observation and allows later review and analysis. Remember, however, that although graphic representation can be helpful in certain situations, the observer may also want to form profiles or determine percentages and ratios that reflect the relative frequency of particular kinds of behavior.

We have not attempted here to list all forms of recording systems useful in educational settings. As you begin to grapple with a variety of observation questions, you will create personal variations.

FIGURE 8.9. **Sample Worksheet B**

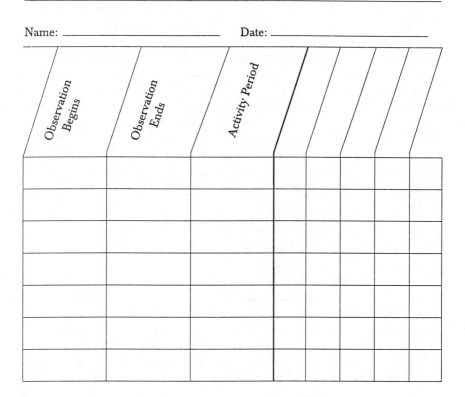

Name: _____   Date: _____

ORGANIZING AND SUMMARIZING OBSERVATIONAL RESULTS

The outcomes of observation have to be organized and summarized so that one can understand such issues as the nature and extent of observed behavior and the effects of instructional or behavioral interventions, and in order to facilitate communication with other professionals and with parents. Observations can be organized and summarized in a number of ways, as we have suggested throughout this book. For example, photos and videos collected over time can be placed in children's portfolios. Checklist records can be maintained with dates recorded when skills are achieved or behaviors of interest demonstrated. Regular logs, maintained over time, can document unfolding skills. The observations included can reflect the natural tasks of children as well as the learning goals and the context in which the skill is demonstrated. Ratings based on judgments collected over time can be compared to help evaluate changes in child behavior, although they provide little help regarding the reasons for a child's behavior or the nature of the context. Running records and video recording can be used to provide comprehensive accounts of behaviors in which the frequency or rate of behavior of interest can be calculated, along with the sequence of events.

When using systematic observational systems, observers can use results in a number of ways depending on the sample collected and the type of procedure used. These include a simple count of the *frequency* with which behaviors of interest occurred or the percentage, rate, or duration of particular behavior(s) during an observation period. The percentage of occurrences of specific behaviors can be calculated by dividing the number of behaviors recorded in each category by the total number of observation opportunities or units. For example, with the information recorded in Figure 8.8, we could determine the percentage of use of each language form across a group of children; that is

$$\frac{\text{Total B, "uses complete sentences"}}{\text{Grand total of all language forms used by all children}}$$

As an example of calculating the rate of behavior, using Figure 8.1, Procedure B, we could divide the total number of L (looking around) behaviors by the 7 time opportunities to find the percentage of time a child spends looking around, or we can calculate change in the duration of events, such as "crying," by using a stopwatch over several observation periods. Importantly, each of these outcomes of observations made across time can be charted and used to document the acquisition of skills, the effects of particular teaching strategies, and the effects that result from intervention.

MAKING VALID OBSERVATIONS

Observational efforts will be in vain if what is observed and recorded does not correspond to real events. First of all, the observer must consider whether the behaviors correspond to the observational purpose. Second, the validity of observations depends on how representative the record is of what actually occurred. Systematic, nonoverlapping categories of behaviors and clear definitions of the behaviors facilitate the objective classification of units of behavior and increase the observer's consistency or reliability. Third, there should be a plan for collecting corroborative observations from others. We might, however, still have an observation record that does not adequately reflect the real world, as evidenced in cases of biased observations. We focus on this important issue by regularly asking:

- What am I trying to sample from the stream of all behavior?
- Why am I interested in the particular information provided by the observation procedures I choose?
- Am I reporting what I see objectively?
- Have unintentional sources of bias been introduced?
- Have I observed long enough and across contexts to obtain a clear picture of the child's behavior?
- Does my recording procedure capture what has happened?

Once again, the particular problem or question raised and the observer's knowledge of that area will affect answers to these questions, and particularly influence the format of the observations made. The validity of our observational measurements of behavior depends at least on these two conditions:

- A representative sample of the behaviors to be measured must be observed.
- A complete, accurate record of the observed behaviors must be made.

In recording and synthesizing observations, while taking into account those procedures that facilitate reliable and valid observations, the major problem that confronts the observer is the observer himself or herself. Drawing conclusions and solving problems demand that observers make inferences after digesting the information gathered during the observation process. Observers relate observations to the variables studied (for example, aggression, anxiety, motivation, and so forth), bringing behavior and construct together by inference. For example, an observer sees a child hitting another child and comes to the conclusion (inference) that the behavior is an example of hostility or aggression. The basic weakness of this process is that incorrect inferences can be made from observations. For example, two or more independent observers will note that in certain neighborhoods white families move out as African-American families move in and infer that property values have gone down. The observation that white families are moving out and African-American families are moving in may be reliable and valid. However, an analysis of property values may show that in fact they have not decreased. Therefore, although certain behavior was observed, the conclusion drawn is invalid and subject to challenge. To judge property values, one should observe the price paid by all families who move in.

Another troublesome issue has to do with the number of observations needed to support our inferences. How often and in what context must a child physically strike another child, for example, before we draw conclusions about the first child's "aggressive" nature or "hostile" manner? Although the answer to this particular question will vary extensively according to the point of view of the observer, the answer will be greatly influenced by the observer's intimate knowledge and understanding of the observed behaviors as well as an appreciation of developmental norms.

Types of Validity

Before inferences and interpretations are arrived at and generalizations made on the basis of observational data, one should consider the various types of validity usually required of other assessment devices and techniques: content-related validity, criterion-related validity (including concurrent and predictive validity), and construct validity. (See Cone, 1982; Hoge, 1985; Kent & Foster, 1977, for additional readings in this area.)

Content-Related Validity. Does the observation procedure (schedule, rating scale, checklist) adequately sample or represent the behavior of concern? Has the observation question been sufficiently refined? Are the categories of observation exhaustive of the problem at hand?

Content validity is a fundamental form of validity for observational procedures. It is important, therefore, to detail the procedures used for developing content validity.

Criterion-Related Validity. Two types of information are used to support criterion-related validity: concurrent and predictive validity. Concurrent validity addresses the question: How do the observed behaviors relate to other external criteria such as test scores, school performance records, other observational data, and parent reports collected at about the same point of time? These concurrent data, independent of the observations, can help substantiate or validate the inference. For example, from observing that a child's distractibility is increased and his or her concentration decreased during unstructured group activities, we might conclude that the child does not respond productively to an unstructured situation. Independent psychological test data might suggest that the child has abilities to attend to detail and concentrate on such tasks as block design or puzzles (subtests on the Wechsler Intelligence Scale for Children—Third Edition, 1991) when these are presented in a one-to-one situation. This finding would provide substantiating evidence that the child is capable of being attentive when placed in the appropriate context or situation. The more independent evidence accumulated to support inferences based on observation, the more credible and valid the inferences become.

Predictive validity addresses the question "How accurately do observational outcomes relate to or predict future performance?" Sources of information at a future time might include teacher observations, test scores, grades, or classroom performance.

Construct Validity. Perhaps the most important question the developer of an observational instrument must ask is: Do the target behaviors observed in fact tap or represent the psychological constructs—for example, "independence," "creativity," "role-taking ability," "intelligence," and so forth—that are of particular interest to the observer? Evidence used to support construct validity is collected over time from multiple sources such as comparisons with other measures of the same construct and studies that document their accuracy in distinguishing individuals or environments of varying levels of development or quality.

The extent and type of validity data to be collected depend on the uses that will be made of the observational information. For example, when data are used to monitor progress in relation to the curriculum, content validity is a major concern. When data are used for purposes of assessment, the observational procedures must document both content- and criterion-related validity.

MAKING INTERPRETATIONS

When we make inferences or draw conclusions from observational data, we are making *interpretations,* or adding meaning to the observations. Interpretations grow out of theories, past experiences, and present observations (McCutcheon, 1981). They "make sense" out of what we see and help us "understand" what we observe. There are at least five kinds of interpretations:

1. Forming *patterns* among observations, such as inferring the apparent order and rules for doing things in a classroom.
2. Interpreting the *social importance and meaning* of observed behaviors: for example, McCutcheon (1981) notes: "We might observe students nodding during [class presentation]. The physical behavior might be described as students moving their heads slightly, in an up and down motion. . . . What does this nodding mean?" (p. 7). The nods may signify different things. Are the pupils following the teacher's thoughts; agreeing with the teacher; feigning an interest that is not there, to be polite; falling asleep; or demonstrating a habit?
3. Relating observations to *external considerations* such as theories, philosophy, and historical events.
4. Relating observations to *developmental data.*
5. Relating observations to the *environment,* both physical components and teacher-based components.

In interpreting observations, one might emphasize one type of interpretation over others. The meaning that comes from interpreting observations grows out of the transaction between what we observe and what we have experienced. Thus, interpretation is in part subjective and in part objective. Interpretations also must have relevance for instructional and behavioral planning and interventions.

DETERMINING THE APPROPRIATENESS
OF AN OBSERVATION SYSTEM

Figure 8.10 gives a list of questions an observer should ask about the observation to be made, the technique to be employed, and its ap-

FIGURE 8.10. Checkpoints for Determining the Appropriateness of an Observational System

1. For what purpose was the system developed?
   A. Does the stated purpose match your goal?
   B. What will be observed (behavioral definition)?
   C. Is the procedure limited by a particular theoretical perspective?

2. Are the conditions for observer reliability met?
   A. Behaviors to be viewed are sufficiently specified so as to be:
      Mutually exclusive (do not overlap each other). Exhaustive (all behaviors of concern can be classified, but the need for exhaustive categories depends on the purpose of a particular observation).
   B. Categories are sufficiently narrow so that two or more observers will place an observed behavior into the same category.
   C. Is observer interpretation necessary or not?
   D. What reliability data are presented?

3. What type of system is employed?
   A. Category system: Every unit of behavior observed is categorized into one of the categories specified.
   B. Sign system: Selected behavioral units, listed beforehand, may or may not actually be observed during a period of time (such as on a checklist, rating scale, or observation schedule).

4. Are appropriate sampling procedures employed?
   A. The procedure for sampling behaviors is systematic:
      Time sampling—occurrence or nonoccurrence of behaviors within specified uniform time units.
      Event sampling—event recorded each time it occurs.
   B. Is the procedure feasible?
      How do you sample individuals to be observed?
      In what period of time?
      Is the desired detail possible given the number of individuals and time units?
   C. What is the coding system like?
      How complex is the system?
      Do tallies or codes require memorization? If coding required, is coding indicated on the record form?
      What is the recording format like?
   D. Are the behaviors to be viewed representative?
      How many behaviors are to be viewed?
      Over what period of time?
      Sampling how many children?

5. Are the conditions for validity met?
   A. Are the behaviors you observe relevant to the inferences and interpretations you make?
   B. Have sources of bias been eliminated?
   C. If existing systems are used, are studies available that document the validity of the system?

6. What training procedures are necessary to learn the system?

7. If studies have been reported using the system, what are their outcomes?

8. What modifications will you have to make to the system to adapt it to your purpose?

9. Have you tried out the system?
   A. Does it capture the particular behaviors in which you are interested?
   B. How easy is it to use and interpret?
   C. Is it culturally sensitive in regard to the groups with whom you are working?

propriateness. After the observer has some experience, these questions should arise as a matter of course, and it will no longer be necessary to consult the checklist.

It is essential for observers to evaluate their observation needs before adopting a published research instrument or observation technique. The array of observation schedules available to the classroom observer often confuses the consumer as to the appropriateness of one structured approach versus another for a given educational situation. Among the most useful resources for helping evaluate a given observational procedure are the *Mirrors for Behavior* anthologies prepared by Simon and Boyer (1967, 1970, 1974), Evertson and Green's chapter in the *Handbook of Research on Teaching* (1986), Foster and Cone's chapter in the *Handbook of Behavioral Assessment* (1986), and Shapiro's *Behavioral Assessment in School Psychology* (1987). Gordon and Jester (1973) have reviewed techniques of observing teaching in early childhood settings, which include home and daycare settings as well as preschool classrooms. Finally, Boyer, Simon, and Karafin (1973) have edited an anthology of early childhood observation instruments.

ETHICAL ISSUES IN OBSERVATION

Given the current climate in which the public has seriously questioned such school activities as psychological testing and other forms of assessment and record-keeping without prior parental permission or knowledge, we must consider the point at which observational techniques may interfere with an individual's privacy and rights. We cannot deny that individuals routinely and legitimately observe each of us in our daily activities. Depending on the nature of the stated purpose of the observation, if someone is observed without being made aware of this or without prior permission, such observations may well constitute an invasion of privacy. In the case of the young child, parental permission is an appropriate consideration. However, as children become more aware of their rights, even though it may affect the results of our data collection, it is necessary to seriously consider informing the child of our intent to observe (Russell Sage Foundation, 1969).

Most classroom observers do not invade a child's privacy. An early childhood specialist observes children as they work in a variety of classroom learning situations in order to develop more effective teaching strategies, and violation occurs only if the data collection goes beyond this function. A student teacher observes in classrooms to gain an understanding of appropriate teaching behaviors and of child development.

The special educator observes the effectiveness of an intervention. The school psychologist observes a child with a behavior problem to better understand the nature of the problem and the classroom conditions that might be contributing factors.

Social scientists, child development researchers, and educators have struggled with the question of privacy and the possible uses to which data can be put, however well-intentioned the observation process may be. The American Psychological Association, in its *Ethical Principles in the Conduct of Research with Human Participants* (1982) (currently being revised) and the Society for Research in Child Development, in a similar report (1982), both stress the rights of the child and the need to respect a child's willingness or refusal to participate in research. Tape recordings, videotapings, and other mechanical recordings—although facilitating the collection of more comprehensive observation information—must be used with such ethical consideration taken into account.

Like most ethical issues, the problem of invasion of privacy through observation techniques is a complex, multifaceted dilemma that cannot be resolved by simple answers (see Brandt, 1972; Fisher & Tyron, 1990). However, as we consider the value of observation skill as a method of inquiry and as a source of building inferences, we must constantly raise the question of ethics. A number of important ethical concerns and procedures for conducting research with children in natural settings, such as informed consent and confidentiality, have been summarized by Rheingold (1982). Also, NAEYC's "Code of Ethical Conduct: Guidelines for Responsible Behavior in Early Childhood Education" (1996) is a more general discussion of standards of ethical behavior in early childhood education.

Since observation is the cornerstone of assessment in early childhood, a number of other concerns should be raised. Among these are the inappropriate use of outcomes, creating false negatives (missing the child who has special needs) or false positives (overidentifying children who do not have special needs), making errors in the interventions suggested, creating a "self-fulfilling prophecy," and producing stigmatizing effects (Adelman & Taylor, 1984).

If observation is carried out systematically over time, many of these concerns can be avoided, for example, collecting a sufficient number of observations to avoid false positives and negatives. However, if observations are going to result in a referral, parental consent is essential. An explanation of what information is being sought and how it will be used is necessary. Of course, parental consent is also required if observations will be made part of a research project.

The Teacher as Observer

Mrs. Paredes, a teacher in a first-grade classroom, is concerned about the behavior of Gregory. He frequently becomes restless and cries in class. In attempting to understand this behavior, Mrs. Paredes decides to observe and record the time of the school day, during what activities, and with what frequency Gregory becomes restless and cries.

The early childhood coordinator observes in the classrooms of new teachers in order to help them meet the needs and interests of handicapped children.

Mrs. Morris, a housemother for young children at a residential treatment center, is concerned with the health and physical care of the eight children for whom she is responsible. Each day of the week she systematically notes physical features of the children such as their skin tone, hair, and fingernails to check that all is in order.

These examples provide us with some notion of the various ways in which observations are used in schools and school-related settings. Now that we have dealt with the major factors involving observation skills and devising observation systems, let us consider some additional issues in using systematic observation techniques in the classroom and developing observation schedules tailored to specific classroom problems (see also Benjamin, 1995).

THE TEACHER OR THE OUTSIDER AS OBSERVER

Although innovations such as team teaching and the use of classroom paraprofessionals have generated possibilities for individuals involved in the classroom to observe ongoing behavior, for the most part systematic observation has been carried out by social workers, school psychologists, researchers, and other school personnel who are not integral members of the classroom setting. Generally, when teachers have used observation techniques, they have been unstructured and highly dependent on remembering the observed behaviors until an opportune time to record them—usually at the end of the day. This situation is rapidly changing as early childhood teachers regularly are called on to engage in systematic observation. Although it is difficult to engage in sustained observation when one is teaching, such observation is important in modifying instruction to meet children's individual needs (see also Barnett & Carey, 1992). The following list presents a number of alternative approaches that can enable the teacher to implement structured and systematic observation procedures in the classroom.

- In collaboration with a team teacher, paraprofessional, or another classroom teacher with a free period, the teacher can develop an appropriate schedule for observing and in turn share observing responsibilities.
- When other personnel are not available, the teacher, again using an appropriate schedule, can decide to depart from the teaching routine and systematically observe during a certain portion of each day. For example, the teacher may decide to observe and record the variety of independent activities engaged in by class members. The observation might take place for 5 minutes at the beginning and 5 minutes at the end of the activities period each day over the course of a week. Children will be engaged in activities while the observation takes place. The amount of time required for observational activity is small in proportion to the benefits that can result from collecting the observation data. For example, to obtain information about the patterns of peer interaction within a classroom, the teacher might decide to observe a sample of five pupils as they interact with classmates; each pupil is observed for 1 minute during each of 4 hours (perhaps 9:00 and 11:00 A.M. and 1:00 and 3:00 P.M.) of the class day over a given number of days.
- The teacher can also function as a "participant-observer," recording observations while interacting with observed pupils. This type of observation, important in early childhood settings, involves the teacher in observing and recording teacher–pupil behaviors in a few predetermined categories over brief periods of time. Or the teacher can make notes regularly while observing emerging behaviors or desired learning outcomes using notecards, checklists, or other formats.

Problems Encountered by the Teacher as Observer

Even when the teacher is removed from the stream of behavior and fulfills the role of observer in the classroom, his or her mere presence in the setting is bound to influence certain pupil behaviors to some extent. One probably would get different results if some other person, such as the principal, were in the classroom.

A more difficult problem, referred to as the "halo effect" (see Unit III), involves the influence of the teacher's previous knowledge and experience with a classroom of pupils and their past behavior on making objective observations of current behavior. For example, from past experience, a teacher, anticipating that Donald is attentive and concentrates well in the classroom, will tend to ignore or underemphasize any instances of "off-task" behavior that Donald exhibits. As another example, many teachers, anticipating that children from lower socioeconomic groups have poor verbal expressive abilities, might overlook instances of excellent verbal expression in the classroom.

One way of tempering the influence of the halo effect is to involve additional independent observers at some point in the observation process to determine how valid the teacher's observations are. The assumption here is that an outside observer has not had previous experience with and expectations of the children involved.

Without question, maintaining regular observation records for each class member is an ongoing challenge that takes time and must be a valued activity in the school. The benefits, however, can make this challenge worthwhile. In addition to being an integral component of developmentally appropriate practice specified by early childhood professional organizations, observational data can be exchanged with support staff and, importantly, with parents, who in turn can be encouraged to share their observations and observe target behaviors at home.

SOLVING CLASSROOM PROBLEMS
THROUGH OBSERVATION TECHNIQUES

We have presented a variety of examples from the classroom in which observation procedures might be used. Let us now consider some general problems that might be approached through observational techniques.

Determining the Effectiveness of Educational Programs and Curricula

Current teacher training programs, the education literature, local school district programs, and the media have exposed teachers to a variety of innovations, theoretical orientations, and ways to deal with day-to-day learning and classroom behavior problems. Observation techniques can facilitate a teacher's adaptation and use of many of these "new" educational ideas. Before introducing a new program intended to produce changes in learning or other classroom behavior, the teacher should collect baseline observation data on behaviors that program is aimed at influencing.

In the example presented in Figure 9.1, we are assuming that a classroom teacher intends to introduce a token reinforcement system aimed at increasing the amount of time the pupils in the class pursue assigned tasks. Before introducing this intervention, it is essential that the

FIGURE 9.1. **Charts for Number of Minutes Each Pupil Worked on Assigned Tasks**

Pupil A

Day	Reading	Arithmetic	Writing	Other Assignments	Total Time Pupil "On Task"	Total Time for Pupil Work on Assigned Tasks
1	20	20	5	10	55	110
2	20	20	4	8	50	120
3	22	18	12	13	65	100
4	25	22	18	19	84	120

Pupil B

Day	Reading	Arithmetic	Writing	Other Assignments	Total Time Pupil "On Task"	Total Time for Pupil Work on Assigned Tasks
1	15	15	10	10	50	110
2	12	17	8	11	48	120
3	18	20	10	7	55	100
4	22	25	15	12	72	120

Double rule indicates baseline

teacher collect observation data on the relevant behavior. The baseline data are collected for days 1 and 2. The token system is introduced on day 3 and continues for a given period of time. The observations should continue to be made during this period to ascertain whether the pupils' on-task behavior has actually changed as a result of the program. Charts such as those shown in Figure 9.1 could be used for recording these observations over a number of days. (We are here showing the results for only 4 days and for only two pupils; an actual reinforcement system and the observations would naturally involve more pupils and a longer observation period.) On-task behavior is defined for this sample as the amount of time pupils work at assigned tasks.

After a sufficient number of days of observation, the teacher could calculate the percentage of on-task behavior for each pupil. This would be the total time the pupil worked divided by the length of working time available. The information recorded on the observation schedule could be transformed into a graph like that shown in Figure 9.2. Here, the total amount of time students could work at all assigned tasks on day 3 was 100 minutes. Pupil A was observed to be on task for a total of 65 minutes. By dividing these 65 minutes by the 100 minutes of total working time we see that pupil A was on task 65% of the time on day 3. By the same method of computation, we found the percentage of on task behavior for day 4, and plotted these figures on the graph. The same procedure was followed for pupil B.

In Figure 9.2, days 1 and 2 yield the baseline information on the percentage of on-task behavior demonstrated by both pupils prior to the introduction of the reinforcement system. If the token program works, the percentage of on-task behavior should increase as the percentages on the graph seem to indicate: From this graph, the teacher could conclude that the on-task behavior of pupils A and B has increased as a result of the token program. To verify this conclusion, the teacher should eliminate the reinforcement system and observe whether there is a decrease in on-task behavior. After confirmation of the reinforcement system's impact on behavior, the teacher would reintroduce the token program, expecting another increase in on-task behavior of the students. (See Alessi & Kay, 1983, and Shapiro, 1978, for additional information about implementing behavioral assessment.)

STUDYING DEVELOPMENTAL DIFFERENCES IN CHILDREN

Observation techniques can provide an effective means of conveying to teachers the basic differences among children at various devel-

FIGURE 9.2. **Graph for Percentage of "On-task" Behavior**

Percent	Day 1	Day 2	Day 3	Day 4	Additional Days of Program
100					
95					
90					
85					
80					
75					
70					
65					
60					
55					
50					
45					
40					

Key: Pupil A: ——   Pupil B: ·········

opmental levels. Often teachers—particularly those just out of teacher training programs—have difficulty setting appropriate expectations and goals for children of different ages in their classes. Making systematic observations of children at successive age levels can provide an effective approach to understanding the behavioral differences demonstrated by children at different ages and track the development of skills in relationship to learning and behavioral goals. For example, although the 3-year-old can be observed having difficulty tying his shoelaces, the 7-year-old child not only performs this task with ease, but also demonstrates facility in many other fine-motor activities. The typical 5-year-old, viewing an airplane in the sky, is unable to describe its real size or rate of speed; however, by 10 years of age, the child is capable of understanding the effects of distance on size and speed. With an appreciation of the basic differences in cognitive, emotional, and motor behaviors of children at different ages, the teacher has a sounder basis on which to base instruction and build curricula.

Diagnostic Assessment of Learning Activity

Certain classroom assessment procedures are variations of systematic event samplings, where the events or problems are presented to each pupil and the teacher observes each pupil's strategy in dealing with them. For example, the teacher may observe each child working on an addition problem involving two-place carrying of numbers, noting that one child has difficulty applying the carrying strategy per se, while another child has difficulty lining up numbers. In order to do such an assessment systematically, the teacher should prepare beforehand a list of relevant learning strategies and errors that can occur on this task and then focus on them in making the observations, as shown in Figure 9.3.

Observing each child perform a task such as the addition problem allows the teacher to view the child's approach to a learning situation, in contrast to the more typical situation in which the child, working alone on his worksheet, might make some errors. In the latter situation, it is difficult to identify why the child had trouble solving the problem. Only through observing the problem-solving process can the teacher know precisely what kind of help a given child might need.

FIGURE 9.3. **Addition of Two-place Problems with Carrying**

Child	Adds where no carrying is required	Lines numbers up correctly	Adds each column separately	Can carry

MAKING CLASSROOM OBSERVATIONS

Following is an overview of the various questions the classroom teacher should consider in developing a useful observation system. In raising these questions, the observer can be aware of the nature of observations and have greater confidence in the inferences and decisions generated as a result of observation activity. An application example follows each question.

1. What is the nature of the problem or the question with which you are confronted? Define the problem and the related behaviors clearly.

> The first-grade teachers at a school located in a large metropolitan area have established a resource center for their pupils. The purpose of the center is to provide an opportunity for the first-graders to engage in a variety of learning activities, focusing on the development of literacy skills in reading and writing. Each of the school's three first-grade classes spends approximately 25 minutes of each day in the center. During this time, the children complete one task that they have individually selected from a series of 30 learning activities: copying shapes, matching letters with objects depicting that letter name, classifying objects into concept categories, listening to an audiotape of a story while looking at pictures of that story, and so on. When a child completes a learning activity and has the project checked by the teacher or aide, the child may choose another task. The teachers want to know if their first-grade pupils are able to select, pursue, and complete these tasks independently of teacher, aide, or other pupil assistance. If assistance is requested, they are also interested in documenting the kinds of assistance provided, such as breaking tasks down into smaller units, directing pupils to a resource, defining a word, offering information, reinforcing attempts, and so forth.
>
> *Problem:* To what extent do individual first-graders select, pursue, and complete the learning activities independently? If assistance is requested, what kinds of teacher prompts are needed?

2. Why should systematic observation be helpful in dealing with this problem or answering the question?

> The teachers decide that by using observational procedures, they will be able to make systematic recording of the pupils' behavior

during their time in the resource center. The teachers could limit their approach to merely looking at completed pupil activities, but by introducing observation of the patterns of pupil behavior in the center and the kinds of assistance needed, the teachers gather a richer pool of information for drawing their conclusions and more directly answering their question about pupil independence. Furthermore, observations over time will provide teachers with an understanding of differences among children in pursuing and completing activities without the assistance of others.

3. What are the relevant characteristics of the setting in which behavior will be observed? (Characteristics of the setting include space, equipment, and people present.)

- What constraints does the physical setting have on possible behaviors?

    Because the average first-grade class at the school consists of 25 children, and since a "standard"-sized classroom has been designated as the resource center, the pupils' behavior is limited in range of mobility. Yet, because of pupil proximity, the setting itself might encourage verbal exchanges and pupils' "assisting" one another. Of course, the availability of the particular learning materials, as opposed to other possible materials, can restrain the scope of behaviors to be viewed.

- What is the physical arrangement of the various components of the setting that might be considered?

    All 30 tasks are numbered and placed in various locations such as bookshelves, window sills, corners of the floor, and on tables. Pupil work areas are provided adjacent to the materials.

- What people will be present in the setting? What characteristics of the individuals or group being observed should be considered?

    In addition to the 25 pupils in the first-grade class, a class teacher, an aide, and an observer are present in the setting. The aide has been trained beforehand in the use of the learning materials and in providing guided assistance when requested to do so by the pupils. The observer will be one of the other first-grade teachers who has arranged a 25-minute free period to coincide with the resource center period of this class.

4. Given the particular focus of your observations and given your knowledge of the problem area, what is the universe of behaviors that you intend to consider?

> The teachers will consider:
>> The pupil's selection of an activity (What task does a pupil choose on any given day? What is the range of tasks that he or she chooses over a period of time?)
>> Engagement with the task (Does the pupil work with or without requesting assistance from teacher, teacher aide, or other pupils?)
>> Requests of assistance and the pupil's response to the assistance
>> When a given task is completed
>
> In addition, it might also be interesting to see if there is a relationship between these observed behaviors and the quality of the pupil's final product.

5. What units of behavior or clearly defined categories of behavior will you focus on?

Analyze the behavior into its component parts. In determining your list of categories for classifying observable behavior, consider whether a previously developed observational schedule might be used. Decide whether a sign or category system is more appropriate for your problem:

Are the categories or signs employed mutually exclusive?

Is the list of categories or signs exhaustive of the universe of behaviors you wish to consider?

> In their search of observational schedules already available for use, the teachers were unable to find a recording system including the categories of behaviors that matched the purpose of their observations.
>
> Since they were interested in evidence of independent behavior, they adopted a sign system; that is, they generated the following specific categories of behavior for labeling observations:
>> The child selects one of the 30 activities, then picks up the materials and takes them to the designated work area. (However, if the child merely looks at the materials without taking them to the work area, this would not be classified as selecting a task.)
>> The child requests assistance from the teacher, aide, or another pupil in the resource center by gesturing for assistance, verbally asking for assistance, or combining gesture and verbal request. (However, if the child asks to get a drink of water or merely talks to the teacher, aide, or another pupil, this would not be classified as a request for assistance.)

The teacher, aide, or other child provides assistance. When providing assistance, the teacher's aide will also note down on an index card the kind of assistance provided.

The child indicates that a given task has been completed by showing the product to the teacher or aide. (However, if the child partially completes the task, he or she would be encouraged to resume work on the task—but this would not constitute a request for assistance.)

6. What sampling procedure (time or event) will most effectively enable you to record representative observations?

    • Will all the people in the setting be observed, or will you select a representative sample?

    The teachers decided which children would be observed and at what frequency. Since it would be impossible for an individual teacher to observe all the children simultaneously, it is necessary to observe a sample of children each day and to order the observations of their behavior systematically. Therefore, the teachers adopted a time sampling procedure—that is, they decided to observe a preselected sample of 5 children each day. Consequently, by the end of a 5–day school week each of the 25 children will have been observed during one of the daily sessions in the resource center.

    • How frequently across time should you observe so that your conclusions have adequate observational support?

    In order to observe each of the 5 children at different points in the work period, the teacher/observer observes each of the 5 children to be observed that day at work for 1 minute during a 5-minute segment. The teacher then proceeds to observe each of the 5 for 1 minute for the second 5–minute segment, and repeats the cycle 2 more times so that each of the 5 children has been observed for a total of 4 minutes. This procedure is followed each day of the week, 5 children at a time, until all 25 children have been observed.

    It is decided to repeat this observation procedure the first week of each month to document student progress and provide feedback to parents.

    • To what extent does the subject of the observation have to be viewed in a variety of settings and activities within the school in order to deal adequately with the particular problem or question? (Does not apply to this particular observation problem.)

7. How should the recording format be designed to be most useful for your observation? (See Figure 9.4 for sample.)

8. How confident are you that your observation schedule facilitates reliable observations? How might you verify this?

> The early childhood coordinator has agreed to help facilitate the project. The teachers have enlisted the help of students from a nearby college to collect observations as a check on reliability. These students can use the information to meet the requirements of a course. A training session is scheduled, and observers practice the use of the observation system.
>
> To determine the reliability of the observational scheme, two of the observers might observe the resource center period on two consecutive days. The degree to which the two raters agreed with each other in recording the instances of request for assistance could then be determined. The percentage of agreement in indicating the pupil's selection of tasks could also be determined by this procedure. A high rate of agreement would indicate a high level of reliability between the observers.

9. What inferences or conclusions can you make on the basis of collected observation data?

> Conclusions can be arrived regarding:
> What tasks were chosen? By how many pupils?
> Which tasks were completed? By how many pupils?
> Were certain chosen tasks completed more often than others?
> How often did pupils request assistance? Which children requested assistance? From whom? What forms of assistance were provided?
> Were there differences among the three classes observed?
> What inferences can be made about the use of the resource center?
> Can the data be summarized in a graph or chart? The use of a graph or chart helps communicate to others the outcomes of observation.

10. Have you realized the goal for which your observations have been made? If not, can you redefine your problem more clearly and focus

FIGURE 9.4. Sample Recording Sheet for Observations in Resource Center

Week 1, Day 1		Child 1	Child 2	Child 3	Child 4	Child 5
Observation Cycle 1 Date:	Activity Selected					
	Form of Assistance Provided* **					
	Response to Assistance					
	Works Independently					
	Completes Task					
Observation Cycle 2 Date:	Activity Selected					
	Form of Assistance Provided					
	Response to Assistance					
	Works Independently					
	Completes Task					
Observation Cycle 3 Date: . . .						
Observation Cycle 4						

* Indicate from whom: Teacher = T
                        Assistant = A
                        Other Child = C

** Forms of assistance such as breaking tasks down into smaller units, directing pupils to a resource, defining a word, offering information, reinforcing attempts, and so forth.

on different behaviors, and from a different perspective? (In other words, can you pilot an alternative approach?)

> The example developed should allow the teachers to answer question #1 above, although alternative approaches to the problem could be developed.

11. Did you consider the role that methods of inquiry other than systematic observation—psychometric testing, controlled experimentation, or developmental histories—might play in dealing with your problem? (Does not pertain to the example presented.)

The Relationship Between Media and Observation

In this unit we will consider briefly the interactions between the observer and the medium of observation. Observation may take place in a live situation or through media—pictures, slides, film, videotape, printed materials, audio recordings, or any combination of these. Increasingly, audio and videotapes are used in classrooms to document child behavior. Each medium has formal characteristics that affect the observation process, and each allows for certain predictions. For example, even the most skilled stenographer is unable to record all the innuendos of a single speaker with paper and pencil, and the task becomes more difficult with an increase in the number of simultaneous speakers. On the other hand, a tape recorder and appropriately placed microphones provide a record of all verbal interactions, even whispers. But the tape system would not pick up gestures or facial expressions. Each medium has its strengths and its limitations, a topic to be covered in greater detail in this unit.

THE "MECHANICS" OF MEDIA AND THE OBSERVER

Several interesting factors should be taken into account when considering the use of media. These include:

- Availability of media equipment
- Ease of use (operation)
- Degree of special training required
- Ease of recording (encoding) and gaining appropriate information from that recording (decoding)
- Range of applicability
- Cost
- Intrusiveness of the media system

For example, paper and pencil are almost always available and require no training for use, but are limited in their applicability without other aids. On the other hand, mechanical sound recording provides a much more complete account of a given situation, but requires costly equipment, which is often inaccessible, necessitates some training to operate, and can intrude on the setting. The question of intrusiveness is important in the choice of media for observational purposes. A behavioral measure of intrusiveness might well be the amount of time required for the subjects of the observation to ignore the presence of the observation system itself.

The still picture or single photograph, while generally easy to obtain, is one of the most difficult observation representations to interpret, due to the minimal sample of behaviors, situations, or actions obtained. The viewer frequently does not know what occurred immediately before or immediately after the incident photographed. Motion picture, by contrast, falls toward the other extreme of the picture-sampling dimension. It normally exposes from 18 to 24 still pictures per second, providing a more complete representation for interpretation. Videotaping, now widely used in classrooms, shares these characteristics. The more complete representation results from the dense sample of situations, behaviors, or actions presented in rapid sequence during a brief span of time. The motion picture or videotape, by presenting many frames per second to the observer, reduces the number of inferences required by the observer.

Actually, more information is available in motion pictures and or videotapes than most viewers use. For example, a frame-by-frame analysis would allow the viewer to look at eye movement. Slow-motion presentation and repeated showings would allow other analyses. The viewer in most film-watching situations does not have time to extract all the information available—in fact, the viewer's perception is usually controlled by the filmmaker or by the purpose for which the film is viewed.

Differences, such as those between the still picture and motion picture, exist among all media and should be considered when choosing among them. The obvious differences of sound, motion, and non-motion occur immediately to most people. The subtle differences, however, also influence the nature of the data.

The ideal observation tool does not yet exist. Such a tool would provide a "magical time machine" display that would allow the observer to be invisible, to control the speed and direction of time, move forward and backward in time, freeze time, and review at will, and have all senses represented. With such a device the observer might well have the sensation of being on the scene without being part of it.

ADVANTAGES AND DISADVANTAGES
OF THE MEDIA OF OBSERVATION

Firsthand Observation

Direct viewing of a given situation provides more information than any individual can deal with at a given time. Therefore, a conscious selection process determines the foci of one's observations. Other information is screened out and what is viewed is ordered to conform with the frames of reference brought to that situation. Thus, an observer concerned about the physical manifestations of nutrition in a group of young children would focus on physical and behavioral features such as skin tone, fingernails, hair, weight, alertness, and energy level, while screening out verbal interchanges between children and the type of objects chosen for play.

The advantages of firsthand observation include:

- The immediacy of the information gained
- The wide range of information available
- The flow of action present (viewer can see, hear, or inquire about what happened immediately prior to or following any given instance)

The advantages of direct observation are also the sources of its limitations:

- The screening out of some behaviors while focusing on others
- The human factor (individual biases or prejudices, memory of events, inappropriate foci)
- The effect of the observer's presence on the events being observed

The presence of more than one trained observer in a given situation can solve some of the problems posed above but introduces others, including cost in time and potential interference with the ongoing process. Thus, the human being without the help of other techniques is restricted in his or her capacity to collect data in a live situation. The introduction of categorized recording systems, rating scales, pictorial records, and sound recordings can strengthen an individual's perceptions. Media of observation are introduced here with an acknowledgment of their strengths and weaknesses. Although no single medium can combine all of the strengths of human observation, various media can be combined and can compensate for some of the weaknesses.

The Still Picture or Slide

A picture or series of pictures, although reflecting the selectivity of the photographer, does permit the viewer to reexamine the picture in order to test his or her own perception and interpretation of that picture. The viewer can examine the order or sequence of behaviors or actions shown to infer, for example, that motion or change took place. The picture or series of pictures also allows the viewer to compare his or her own observations with those made by others of the same events, and to review the depicted events at some future time. The observation process can thus be extended beyond the limitations of the observing human being. The ability to review the stimuli provides the primary advantage of the single still picture or sequence of pictures over direct observation.

The major limitation of a single picture or slide is the obvious one: It presents a static view of the instance, forcing the viewer to seek additional information or to make inferences without knowing what immediately preceded or followed the event. A second limitation is that in most cases the photographer makes the selection for the viewer. It might be useful to contrast viewing a still picture and a painting: An individual looking at a painting tends to seek subtle meaning in it, whereas the same individual viewing a photograph often accepts it as total reality, when it is in fact a partial representation of reality. One way to deal with this problem is to use a sequence of still pictures. Each additional picture, in sequence, clarifies the scene, setting, interactions, and outcomes.

The teacher, then, may find a "before" and "after" photo useful, or may wish to photograph a sequence of events to capture a developmental milestone or a project to place in a child's portfolio. The collection of photos over time can be useful in documenting children's emerging skills and in communicating learning outcomes with parents. Photographic surveys of classrooms can provide teachers with detailed understanding of classroom environments. Adis (1977), for example, used a photographic survey to identify patterns of student interaction with classroom resources. Photographs of classrooms were taken and coded through use of a locational grid and computerized blueprint of each classroom. Thus it was possible to track patterns of student interaction with classroom resources and other students. Additional simple recordings can involve photographing each activity area of the room and the classroom clock on a regular basis during a day—for example, every 15 minutes during an entire school day.

Audio Recordings

When one has adequate equipment and appropriately placed microphones, audiotape recordings can provide a flexible record of verbal interchanges in a situation. To evaluate a conversation one might focus on content analysis, phonemic analysis, volume-level shift, pacing, and expression. In the live situation the hearer/observer would never be able to absorb and analyze the conversation from these varied foci. The recording, because of its *playback* characteristic, allows for other analyses, and for this reason is a major item in the repertoire of observation tools.

When sound recordings are transcribed, considerable information is lost, for the innuendos of expression, pace, and intonation are difficult to retain once the conversation is in typescript. Audio recordings alone also have limitations in comparison with pictorial recordings. There is loss of information obtained from facial expressions or body movements (which might be in contrast to what is spoken), the behaviors of others, and the setting. The level of noise in active early childhood classrooms presents a challenge for clear recording. However, if notes regarding the context are made, the value of audio recordings is greatly enhanced. Also, on the positive side of the coin, the transcriptions can be reviewed and recorded in an objective manner. In combination with other media, sound recording contributes to the completeness of the recorded representation.

Films and Videotapes

A 16mm sound film or a videotape provides the most complete recording of most situations, since auditory, visual, and time dimensions are accounted for, but the observer tends to be more passive while viewing film and is subject to the selectivity of the filmmaker. Furthermore, there is ample room for viewer selectivity to come into play, for viewers will bring their own biases, training, and experiences to viewing the film. Sound film has the specific advantages of high density and flexibility: Film and videotape can be viewed frame by frame, stopped at a given frame, replayed, and reviewed by many observers. Therefore, this is a very useful form both for purposes of training and for analyzing data. Use of computer analysis facilitates highly detailed accounts of behavior. Interactive videodiscs further enhance the use of observational sequences.

The major limitations to the use of sound film and videotape derive from the cost and the technical competency required for quality production. Recent advances in technology have eliminated some of these problems. Schools increasingly have videotape equipment that can be borrowed for classroom use. Observers using videotapes need to keep in mind, however, that important behaviors can still be missed, depending on the angle of the camera and the activity of the child. Young children move frequently and do not necessarily face the camera. Equipment can break down, the noise level of a room might be high, or one can forget to turn the camera on.

Despite these cautions, film and videotape can greatly enhance our understanding of young children, including the processes and strategies they use to solve problems. Kounin (1975), for example, videotaped child behaviors both in free play and in formal lesson settings. Teachers' communication styles, use of materials and visual aids, and pupil behaviors such as listening and responding to a story all influenced the success of lessons. Ginsburg (1987) has used videotape to investigate young children's understanding of number. He has developed teacher workshop packages built around these videotapes that focus on strategies children use to solve number problems, the kinds of errors they make, and how they explain these errors. Following a child's response, an interviewer poses questions such as "How did you figure out your answer?" or "How did you know?" Although the child might respond "Because I am smart," important clues may be revealed from the tape regarding the child's skills. Teachers and parents can develop considerable insight through observing and discussing such videotaped sequences. Also, video is being used to record changes that occur when special programs are introduced, such as parents' interactions around book reading in intergenerational literacy programs (Brobst & Boehm, 1993; Whitehurst et al., 1994).

Black-and-White or Color

We live in a chromatic world and when we view situations firsthand, the chromatic qualities are of course retained. The degree to which visual media can reproduce the chromatic qualities of firsthand observations varies. Color reproductions have a different information-carrying capacity than black-and-white productions. For example, look again at the photograph of the supermarket scene for Task 2 near the start of Unit IV and consider the additional information a color reproduction might have provided about the store, for example, about the specific products available or purchased. Color carries information, but it can also dominate the viewer's perceptions and, depending on one's purposes, may need to be screened out.

Mechanical Recording Systems

Counting devices, not unlike portable calculators, are available for recording the frequency of behaviors of interest. Microcomputer systems also allow the collection of data about individuals as they respond to program materials—concerning reaction time, errors made, branching, and the number of attempts to meet a criterion level.

In summary, the observer must consider carefully the characteristics, advantages, and drawbacks of different media forms with the end of maintaining as much control as possible. Kent and Foster (1977) make the point that different media forms may not be equivalent or even comparable since they produce different kinds of data. However, the use of both audiotape and videotape or film greatly enhances our ability to review carefully the observation situation. Unless these media are an integral component of the environment, however, their introduction may be intrusive. A period of time to adjust to the presence of these nonhuman observers may be necessary.

The effects of different media on the resulting observational data have been summarized by Foster and Cone (1986), who point out that:

- Interobserver agreement differs between live observation and when observing videotaped presentations. Depending on the target behaviors observed, agreement tends to be higher in live situations.
- Findings are not uniform across media.

Conclusion

In this book we have highlighted the role that systematic observation in natural settings may play in approaching problems and facilitating educational programs in classroom and other learning environments. Yet the astute observer should not accept naturalistic observation methodology exclusively over other methods of inquiry into educational processes. Although feelings and attitudes underlie many behaviors, it is often impossible to understand these dimensions through direct observation. Interviewing and self-report questionnaires may be more effective means of tapping these areas. For example, evaluating a child's self-esteem might be more directly approached through alternative methods of study. Moreover, since certain behaviors rarely occur in naturalistic situations, it may be necessary to create an experimental or testing situation in order to study—or observe—such behaviors as problem-solving strategies, patterns of discovery, learning, and divergent thinking.

As one of a variety of methodological tools, systematic observation can help the practitioner unravel and understand the complex behavioral exchanges among participants in various learning contexts. Developing and using observation techniques and interpreting the results of systematic observing are complex activities, yet with increased experience, the trained observer will be able to generate useful information on the basis of direct observation.

Furthermore, we would like to suggest that there is no one best way of observing. Each observer must define an area of concern and choose those methods most appropriate to the problem being confronted as well as to his or her own style of working. It is hoped that this guide has provided the observer with a flexible yet systematic orientation for collecting and using observational data as vital sources of information in educational decision making.

Perhaps the most active of all classroom observers is the child. It is well known that children learn what to expect from their teachers and parents, and to a large extent this information is gathered through observing what happens from day to day. Furthermore, observation is essential to children's intellectual and social growth, as they assimilate and accommodate to information from their environment. There is no reason why children should not be guided in the use of systematic observation strategies by defining observation problems, observing objectively, and supporting inferences with data. In fact, such an approach is a curricular emphasis of some recent science education programs.

Carrying this point one step further, why not also train secondary school pupils to help us collect some of the observational data required for making appropriate educational decisions? The next generation of well-trained observers sits in the classroom.

Finally, the classroom observer of young children usually will find it productive to collaborate with the parent as observer. Understanding and building on children's experiences across many contexts of course must involve the home. Parents are a valuable resource for the classroom observer in numerous ways. Parents can provide essential information about their child's typical behavior at home or in settings outside of school. Parents can also be trained as observers or co-observers focusing on the same developmental areas as do teachers and providing corroborating information or new observational information. When a problem arises, the parent and teacher can use observation as a means of identifying and working through problems, and, as a result, foster home-school collaboration.

Sample Responses to Tasks

Sample Responses to Task 1

Observations of Your Present Setting (5-Minute Time Limit)

Setting: A classroom where students and instructor are gathered.

Time of Day: 2:00 P.M. (Class began at 1:45)

Observer: A

Observations in Sequence

1. The room is cold.

2. There are more women than men in this room.

3. I can hear adult voices.

4. There are white cabinets in this room.

5. The blackboard looks gray.

6. Quiet room.

7. Tables give room for work.

8. Large windows, high ceiling—good ventilation.

9. Age of people seems to range from early 20s to middle 30s.

10. This room seems to be connected to another.

11. Most of the people are busy writing.

Sample Responses to Task 1 (continued)

Observer: B

Observations in Sequence

1. Young teacher.

2. Wooden ledge under blackboard.

3. Faces—some tired, some absorbed.

4. It's quiet.

5. Group is sitting in semicircle.

6. Everyone is looking around and writing.

7. Surprised class is so small.

8. Informal and relaxed atmosphere.

Observer: C

Observations in Sequence

1. High ceiling in room.

2. Bright-colored and beige walls.

3. The room is approximately square.

4. Several tables and chairs.

5. A group of about 12 people.

6. Most of the people are busy writing.

7. The room adjoins another where some people are talking.

Sample Responses to Task 4

Observations of a Girl in a Head Start Classroom

Observations Made	Inferences Drawn	Observations Supporting Inferences (#1, #2)
1. She is sitting alone on a pile of blocks.	A. The child is not interacting with other children.	A. 1, 2
2. Other children in the block area are not focusing their attention on her.	B. The child is fearful of playing along with active young children.	B. 1, 3, 4
3. At least two of the four are involved (actively?) in play with blocks.	C. The child is resting briefly after having played with the boys in the block area.	C. 1
4. She is looking away from the other children and their activities. (We do not know what she is looking at.)	D. The child is role-playing an "actress" who has received a bouquet of flowers.	D. 1, 5
5. She is holding a bouquet of flowers.		

Sample Responses to Task 5

Differentiating Clearly Stated from Poorly Stated Questions

Question	Well Stated	Poorly Stated	Reason
1. Are boys more restless than girls during small-group "big book" activities?		✓	What is meant by the word "restless"? The question should be restated to direct the observer's attention to specific behaviors.*
2. Does the teacher in this classroom encourage questioning behavior?		✓	What behavior is implied by the word "encourage"? The question should be restated so that "encourage" is more clearly defined in terms of specific behaviors.†
3. During a given kindergarten class day, how many individual children choose to look at a book during free play?	✓		The observer could generate a system for counting the number of children looking at books during the time indicated.
4. Why do the girls in the kindergarten class appear to be more motivated to clean up after snack time?		✓	What is meant by the word "motivated"? The question should be restated so that "motivated" is more clearly defined in terms of specific behaviors.§

---

* - "Do boys leave their chairs during small-group activities or turn away from the reading-readiness group and appear to attend to other activities more frequently than do girls in this setting?" Or,
- "Does the teacher reprimand boys more frequently than girls during small-group activities?"
† - "How often does the teacher nod, smile, give verbal recognition, or other social reinforcers to pupils after they have asked questions?"
§ - "Do girls self-initiate cleaning of the table, replacing utensils, etc., more often than boys?"

140

Sample Responses to Task 6

Constraints Imposed by the Setting

Category	Characteristics	Unlikely Behaviors	Likely Behaviors
1. People	Two adults: one appears to be observing; the other appears to be associated with the group (sex difficult to determine) White and black young boys and girls dressed for warm weather.	Behavior reflecting children's social interaction with adults who are older than the two present in the play area	Behavior reflecting children's exchanges with black and white, same-sex and opposite-sex peers and accessible adults; Observations of ongoing behavior Children's mobility facilitated by lack of bulky clothing
2. Materials Available	Hard surface on path Grass 1 wagon, 2 tricycles, and 1 tricycle-wagon 1 guitar 3 bushes visible	The lack of typical playground equipment eliminates possibility of activities such as climbing, swinging, sliding	Bicycle-riding, wagon-pulling, unrestricted running and jumping Trying out a guitar and singing Possible games such as "hide and seek"
3. Space	Large open area		Many simultaneous activities
4. Other Features (indicate)			

Sample Responses to Task 9

Distinguishing Mutually Exclusive Categories

Categories	Mutually Exclusive	Overlapping

1. running
   lying prone
   sitting in place
   standing in place
	✓	

2. laughing
   crying
   talking
		✓

3. reading
   looking
   listening
		✓

4. asking a question
   giving a command
   stating an opinion
	✓	

In Task 9, example 1 and 4 are clusters of mutually exclusive categories because an observed behavior could never be classified in more than one of the indicated categories. However, examples 2 and 3 have overlapping categories—an individual can cry and talk simultaneously and, other than in the instance of "reading" braille, one cannot read a book without looking at it.

Sample Responses to Task 10

Categories of Large-muscle Coordination Playground Activity

1. Crawling	6. Running
2. Walking	7. Climbing
3. Jumping	8. Throwing a ball
4. Skipping	9. Riding a bicycle
5. Dancing	10. Other*

*To be specified by the observer at each observation session.

Sample Responses to Task 11
Determining Representative Observational Samples

Problem or Question	Behavior Sample	Representative? Yes	Representative? No	Reasons for Your Response
Study of first-grade children's "on-task" behavior in school.	Observe the behavior of children sitting in a front-row seat of each row in a particular class.		✓	• Not random sampling: Front row might include only children with visual or behavioral problems, etc. • Only one class: This class might not be representative of the entire first-grade population of the school because of an achievement group, teacher influence, or other factors.
Count of out-of-seat behaviors of an "acting-out" kindergartner.	Observe the child on 5 successive days from 10:00 A.M. to 10:15 A.M.		✓	• One might question 5 successive days, not necessarily spread out over enough time. • Activities during 10:00 to 10:15 might be the same each day, e.g., only group sessions might have been observed. One needs to sample activities at other times of the day.
Study the extent to which 5-year-old children interact in same-sex, opposite-sex, or mixed-sex groupings on the playground.	Randomly choose four boys and four girls. Observe each child's behavior on a systematic rotation basis for 5 minutes, indicating the amount of time each child interacts in designated categories. Sampling should be done on different days and at different times.	✓		• Random choice of boys and girls. • Observed on different days to avoid problem of unrepresentative sample of days. • If possible, different times to avoid such factors as fatigue or hunger. • Since interest is in playground interaction only, observation in other settings is eliminated.

References

Adelman, H. S., & Taylor, L. (1984). Ethical concerns and identification of psychoeducational problems. *Journal of Clinical Child Psychology, 13* (1), 16–23.

Adis, W. (1977). *A photographic analysis of the classroom environment.* New York: Metropolitan School Study Council Exchange, Teachers College, Columbia University, *35* (8).

Ainsworth, M. D. S., Blehar, M., Waters, E., & Wall, S. (1978). *Patterns of attachment.* Hillsdale, NJ: Erlbaum.

Alessi, G. J., & Kaye, J.H. (1983). *Behavior assessment for school psychologists.* Kent, OH: National Association of School Psychologists.

Almy, M., & Genishi, C. (1981). *Ways of studying children* (rev. ed.). New York: Teachers College Press.

American Psychological Association. (1982). *Ethical principles in the conduct of research with human participants.* Washington, DC: Author.

Bagnato, S. J., & Neisworth, J. T. (1992). *Assessment for early intervention.* New York: Guilford.

Bailey, D. B. (1989). Assessing environments. In D. B. Bailey & M. Wolery (Eds.), *Assessing infants and preschoolers with handicaps* (pp. 97–118). Columbus, OH: Merrill.

Baker, E. H., & Tyne, T. F. (1980, Fall). The use of observational procedures in school psychological services. *School Psychology Monograph, 4* (1), 25–44.

Baldwin, A. L. (1968). *Theories of child development.* New York: Wiley.

Bandura, A. (1978). The self system in reciprocal determinism. *American Psychologist, 33,* 344–358.

Bandura, A., & Walters, R. H. (1963). *Social learning and personality development.* New York: Holt, Rinehart & Winston.

Barker, R. G. (1968). *Ecological psychology.* Stanford, CA: Stanford University Press.

Barker, R. G., & Schoggen, P. (1973). *Qualities of community life.* San Francisco: Jossey-Bass.

Barker, R. G., & Wright, H. F. (1951). *One boy's day: A specimen record of behavior.* New York: Harper & Row.

Barker, R. G., & Wright, H. F. (1955). *Midwest and its children: The psychological ecology of an American town.* New York: Harper & Row.

Barnett, D. W., & Carey, K. T. (1992). *Designing interventions for preschool learning and behavior problems.* San Francisco: Jossey-Bass.

Barnett, D. W., & MacMann, G. M. (1992). Decision reliability and validity:

Contributions and limitations of alternative assessment strategies. *The Journal of Special Education, 25,* 431–452.

Baumrind, D. (1968). *Naturalistic observation in the study of parent–child interaction.* Paper presented at the 76th Annual American Psychological Association Convention, September.

Beaty, J. J. (1993). *Observing development of the young child* (3rd ed.). New York: Macmillan.

Beecher, R. (1973). *Teacher approval and disapproval of classroom behavior in prekindergarten, kindergarten, and first grade.* Unpublished doctoral dissertation, Teachers College, Columbia University, New York.

Benjamin, A. (1995). Observation in early childhood classrooms: Advice from the field. *Young Children, 49* (6), 14–20.

Bloom, B. S., Hastings, J. T., & Madaus, G. F. (1971). *Handbook on formative and summative evaluation of student learning.* New York: McGraw-Hill.

Boehm, A. E. (1973). Criterion referenced assessment for the teacher. *Teachers College Record, 75,* 117–126.

Boehm, A. E., & Brassard, M. R. (in press). *Preschool assessment: Strategies and tools.* New York: Guilford.

Boice, R. (1983). Observational skills. *Psychological Bulletin, 93* (1), 3–29.

Boyer, E. G., Simon, A., & Karafin, G. R. (Eds.). (1973). *Measures of maturation: An anthology of early childhood observation instruments.* Philadelphia: Research for Better Schools.

Bradley, R. H. (1982). The home inventory: A review of the first fifteen years. In N. Anastasiow, W. Frankenburg, & A. Fandal (Eds.), *Identifying the developmentally delayed child.* Baltimore: University Park Press.

Bramlett, R. K., & Barnett, D. W. (1993). The development of a direct observation code for use in preschool settings. *School Psychology Review, 22,* 49–62.

Brandt, R. (1972). *Studying behavior in natural settings.* New York: Holt, Rinehart & Winston.

Bredekamp, S. (Ed.). (1987). *Developmentally appropriate practice in early childhood programs serving children from birth through age 8.* Washington, DC: National Association for the Education of Young Children.

Brobst, K. E., & Boehm, A. E. (1993, November). *Using children's book genres to teach parents cognitive reading strategies.* Poster presented at the Second National Head Start Conference, Washington, DC.

Bronfenbrenner, U. (1977). Toward an experimental ecology of human development. *American Psychologist, 32,* 513–531.

Bronfenbrenner, U. (Ed.). (1979). *The ecology of human development: Experiments by nature and design.* Cambridge, MA: Harvard University Press.

Brown, R. A. (1973). *First language: The early stages.* Cambridge, MA: Harvard University Press.

Bruner, J., Goodnow, J., & Austin, G. (1956). *A study of thinking.* New York: Wiley.

Bryant, D. M., Clifford, R. M., & Peisner, E. S. (1991). Best practices for beginners: Developmental appropriateness in kindergarten. *American Educational Research Journal, 28*, 783–803.

Caldwell, B. M. (1969). A new "approach" to behavioral ecology. In J. P. Hill (Ed.), *Minnesota symposium on child psychology* (vol.2, pp. 74–109). Minneapolis: University of Minnesota Press.

Caldwell, B. M., & Bradley, R. H. (1979). *Home observation for measurement of the environment.* Little Rock: Center for Child Development and Education, University of Arkansas at Little Rock.

Cantrell, M. L., & Cantrell, R. P. (1985). Assessment of the natural environment. *Education and Treatment of Children, 8*, 275–295.

Carta, J. J., Greenwood, C. R., & Atwater, J. (1985). *Ecobehavioral System for Complex Assessment of the Preschool Environment (ESCAPE).* Kansas City, KA: Juniper Gardens Children's Project, Bureau of Research, University of Kansas.

Cartwright, G. A., & Cartwright, G. P. (1984). *Developing observational skills* (2nd ed.). New York: McGraw-Hill.

Charlesworth, W. (1978). Ethology: Understanding the other half of intelligence. *Social Science Information (Sage Publications), 17* (2), 231–277.

Cohen, D. H., Stern, V., & Balaban, N. (1996). *Observing and recording the behavior of young children* (4th ed.). New York: Teachers College Press.

Cone, J. D. (1982). Validity of direct observation assessment procedures. In D. P. Hartmann (Ed.), *Using observers to study behavior.* San Francisco: Jossey-Bass.

Dunst, C. J., McWilliam, R. S., & Holbert, R. (1986). Assessment of preschool classroom environments. *Diagnostique, 11*, 212–232.

Education for All Handicapped Children Act of 1975, 20 U.S.C. 1401. (1975).

Education of the Handicapped Act Amendments of 1986, Part H—Handicapped Infants and Toddlers, 101, 20 U.S.C. 1400. (1986).

Education of the Handicapped Act Amendments of 1990, 20 U.S.C. 1400. (1990).

Elliot, S. N., Busse, R. T., & Gresham, F. M. (1993). Behavior rating scales: Issues of use and development. *School Psychology Review, 22*, 313–321.

Evertson, C. M., & Green, J. L. (1986). Observation as inquiry and method. In M. C. Wittrock (Ed.), *Handbook of research on teaching* (3rd ed., pp. 162–213). New York: Macmillan.

Fassnacht, G. (1982). *Theory and practice of observing behavior.* New York: Academic Press.

Fewell, R. R. (1984). Assessment of preschool handicapped children. *Educational Psychologist, 19* (3), 172–179.

Fisher, C. B., & Tryon, W. W. (Eds.). (1990). *Ethics in applied developmental psychology: Emerging issues in an emerging field.* Norwood, NJ: Ablex Publishing Corporation.

Flanders, N. A. (1965). *Teacher influence, pupil attitudes, and achievement* (monograph no. 12). Washington, DC: U.S. Office of Education.

Flanders, N. A. (1970). *Analyzing teacher behavior*. Reading, MA: Addison-Wesley.

Flanders, N. A. (1975). The use of interaction analyses to study pupil attitudes toward learning. In R. Weinberg & F. Wood (Eds.), *Observation of pupils and teachers in mainstream and special education settings: Alternative strategies* (pp. 41–74). Minneapolis: U.S.O.E. Leadership Training Institute/Special Education.

Foster, S. I., & Cone, J. D. (1986). Design and use of direct observation procedures. In A. R. Ciminero, K. S. Calhoun, & E. E. Adams (Eds.), *Handbook of behavioral assessment* (2nd ed., pp. 234–253). New York: Wiley.

Furuno, S., et al. (1979). *The Hawaii early learning profile*. Palo Alto, CA: VORT Corporation.

Gagné, R. M. (1985). *The conditions of learning*. New York: Holt, Rinehart & Winston.

Genishi, C. (Ed.). (1992). *Ways of assessing children and curriculum*. New York: Teachers College Press.

Ginsburg, H. P. (1987). *Assessing the arithmetic abilities and instructional needs of students*. Austin, TX: Pro-Ed.

Gitler, D., & Gordon, R. (1979). Observing and recording young handicapped children's behavior: A comparison among observational methodologies. *Exceptional Children, 2,* 134–135.

Glaser, R., & Nitko, A. J. (1971). Measurement in learning and instruction. In R. L. Thorndike (Ed.), *Educational measurement* (pp. 625–670). Washington, DC: American Council on Education.

Glutting, J. J., McDermott, P. A., & Oakland, T. (1989). Observing child behavior during testing: Constructs, validity, and situational generality. *Journal of School Psychology, 27,* 155–164.

Good, T. L., & Brophy, J. E. (1970). Teacher–child dyadic interactions: A new method of classroom observation. *Journal of School Psychology, 8,* 131–138.

Good, T. L., & Brophy, J. E. (1991). *Looking in classrooms* (5th ed.). New York: HarperCollins.

Gordon, I. J., & Jester, R. E. (1973). Techniques of observing teaching in early childhood and outcomes of particular procedures. In R. M. W. Travers (Ed.), *Second handbook of research on teaching* (pp. 184–217). Chicago: Rand McNally.

Greenwood, C. R., & Carta, J. J. (1987). An ecobehavioral interaction analysis of instruction within special education. *Focus on Exceptional Children, 19,* 3–13.

Gronlund, N. E. (1985). *Measurement and evaluation in teaching* (5th ed.). New York: Macmillan.

Harms, T., & Clifford, R. M. (1980). *Early Childhood Environment Rating Scale*. New York: Teachers College Press.

Harms, T., & Clifford, R. M. (1989). *Family Day Care Rating Scale*. New York: Teachers College Press.

Harms, T., & Clifford, R. M. (1993). Studying educational settings. In B. Spodek

(Ed.), *Handbook of research on the education of young children* (pp. 477–492). New York: Macmillan.

Harms, T., Cryer, D., & Clifford, R. M. (1990). *Infant/Toddler Environment Rating Scale.* New York: Teachers College Press.

Harms, T., Jacobs, E. V., & White, D. R. (1996). *School-Age Care Environment Rating Scale.* New York: Teachers College Press.

Hartmann, D. P. (1982). Assessing the dependability of observational data. In D. P. Hartmann (Ed.), *Using observers to study behavior* (pp. 51–65). San Francisco: Jossey-Bass.

Heller, K., Holtzman, W., & Messick, S. (1982). *Placing children in special education: A strategy for equity.* Washington, DC: National Academy Press.

High/Scope Educational Research Foundation. (1992). *High/Scope Child Observation Record Manual.* Ypsilanti, MI: High/Scope Press.

Hills, T. W. (1993). Assessment in context—Teachers and children at work. *Young Children, 48* (5), 20–28.

Hobbs, N. (1978). Families, schools, and communities: An ecosystem for children. *Teachers College Record, 79* (4), 756–766.

Hoge, R. D. (1985). The validity of direct observation measures of pupil classroom behavior. *Review of Educational Research, 55* (4), 469–483.

Hohmann, M., Banet, B., & Weikart, D. P. (1979). *Young children in action: A manual for preschool educators.* Ypsilanti, MI: High/Scope Press.

Hollenbeck, A. R. (1978). Problems of reliability in observational research. In G. D. Sackett (Ed.), *Observing behavior, vol. II: Data collection and analyses methods* (pp. 79–98). Baltimore: University Park Press.

Irwin, D. M., & Bushnell, M. M. (1980). *Observational strategies for child study.* New York: Holt, Rinehart & Winston.

Jablon, J. R., Marsden, D. B., & Meisels, S. J. (1993). *The Work Sampling System omnibus guidelines for the developmental checklists.* Ann Arbor, MI: Rebus Planning Associates.

Joyce, B., & Weil, M. (1972). *Models of teaching.* Englewood Cliffs, NJ: Prentice-Hall.

Kagan, J., & Kogan, N. (1970). Individual variation in cognitive processes. In P. H. Mussen (Ed.), *Carmichael's handbook of child psychology.* New York: Wiley.

Kaplan, C. (1993). Reliability and validity of test-session behavior observations: Putting the horse before the cart. *Journal of Psychoeducational Assessment, 11,* 314–322.

Kaufman, M., Agard, J. A., & Semmel, M. I. (1985). *Mainstreaming: Learners and their environment.* Cambridge, MA: Brookline Books.

Kazdin, A. E. (1982). Observer effects: Reactivity of direct observation. In D. P. Hartmann (Ed.), *Using observers to study behavior* (pp. 5–20). San Francisco: Jossey-Bass.

Kemp, M. (1987). *Watching children read and write: Observational records for children with special needs.* Portsmouth, NH: Heinemann.

Kent, R. N., & Foster, S. L. (1977). Direct observational procedures: Methodological issues in naturalistic settings. In A. R. Ciminero, K. S. Calhoun, & H. E. Adams (Eds.), *Handbook of behavioral assessment* (pp. 279–328). New York: Wiley.

Keogh, B. K. (1972). Psychological evaluation of exceptional children: Old hangups and new directions. *Journal of School Psychology, 10,* 141–145.

Kerlinger, F. N. (1964, 1973, & 1986). *Foundations of behavioral research.* New York: Holt, Rinehart & Winston.

Kleinmuntz, B. (1967). *Personality measurement.* Homewood, IL: Dorsey Press.

Kogan, N. (1983). Stylistic variation in childhood and adolescence: Creativity, metaphor, and cognitive style. In P. H. Mussen (Ed.), *Handbook of child psychology* (4th ed., vol. 3, pp. 630–706). New York: Wiley.

Kounin, J. S. (1975). An ecological approach to classroom activity settings: Some methods and findings. In R. A. Weinberg & F. H. Wood (Eds.), *Observation of pupils and teachers in mainstream and special education settings* (pp. 149–158). Minneapolis: U.S.O.E. Leadership Training Institute/Special Education.

Kowatrakul, S. (1959). Some behaviors of elementary school children related to classroom activities and subject areas. *Journal of Educational Psychology, 50,* 121–128.

Lambert, N. M., Windmiller, M., Cole, L. S., & Tharinger, D. (1981). *AAMD Adaptive Behavior Scale—school edition.* Monterey, CA: Publishers Test Service, CTB/McGraw-Hill.

Landesman-Dwyer, S., Stein, J. G., & Sackett, G. P. (1978). A behavioral and etiological study of group homes. In G. P. Sackett (Ed.), *Observing behaviors,* Vol. 1: *Theory and applications in mental retardation* (pp. 349–378). Baltimore: University Park Press.

Lentz, F. E., Jr., & Shapiro, E. S. (1986). Functional assessment of the academic environment. *School Psychology Review, 15,* 346–357.

Lidz, C. S. (1991). *Practitioner's guide to dynamic assessment.* New York: Guilford.

Linder, T. (1993a). *Transdisciplinary play-based assessment: A functional approach to working with young children* (Rev. ed.). Baltimore: Paul H. Brookes.

Linder, T. (1993b). *Transdisciplinary play-based intervention: Guidelines for developing a meaningful curriculum for young children.* Baltimore: Paul H. Brookes.

Lynch, E. W., & Hanson, M. J. (1992). *Developing cross-cultural competence: A guide for working with young children and their families.* Baltimore: Paul H. Brookes.

Lytton, H. (1971). Observation studies of parent–child interaction: A methodological review. *Child Development, 42,* 651–684.

Mann, J., Ten Have, T., Plunkett, J. W., & Meisels, S. J. (1991). Time sampling: A methodological critique. *Child Development, 62,* 227–241.

Martin, J. (1976). Developing category observation instruments for the analysis of classroom behavior. *Classroom Interaction Newsletter, 12* (1), 5–16.

Martuza, V. R. (1977). *Applying norm-referenced and criterion-referenced measurement in education.* Boston: Allyn and Bacon.

Masling, J., & Stern, G. (1969). The effect of the observer in the classroom. *Journal of Educational Psychology, 60,* 351–354.

McCloskey, G. (1990). Selecting and using early childhood rating scales. *Topics in Early Childhood Special Education, 10,* 39–64.

McCutcheon, G. (1981). On the interpretation of classroom observations. *Educational Researcher, 10* (5), 5–10.

McGrew, W. C. (1972). *An ethological study of children's behavior.* New York: Academic Press.

McWilliam, R. A., & Dunst, C. J. (1985). *Needs Evaluation for Educators of Developmentally Delayed Students (NEEDS).* Unpublished rating scale. Morganton, NC: Family, Infant and Preschool Program (Western Carolina Center).

Mead, M. (1932). *Coming of age in Samoa.* New York: Morrow.

Medley, D. M., & Mitzel, H. E. (1963). Measuring classroom behavior by systematic observation. In N. L. Gage (Ed.), *Handbook of research in teaching* (pp. 247–328). Chicago: Rand McNally.

Moore, G. T. (1987). The physical environment and cognitive development in child-care centers. In C. S. Weinstein & T. G. David (Eds.), *Spaces for children: The built environment and child development* (pp. 41–72). New York: Plenum.

Morrow, L. M. (1991). Relationship among physical design of play centers, teachers' emphasis on literacy in play, and children's literacy behaviors during play. In *40th yearbook: National Reading Conference* (pp. 127–140). Chicago.

National Association for the Education of Young Children. (1996). NAEYC's code of ethical conduct: Guidelines for responsible behavior in early childhood education. *Young Children* (March), 57–60.

National Association for the Education of Young Children (NAEYC) and National Association of Early Childhood Specialists in State Department of Education (NAECS/SDE). (1991). Guidelines for appropriate curricular content and assessment in programs for serving children ages 3 through 8. *Young Children, 46* (3), 21–38.

Neisworth, J. T., & Bagnato, S. J. (1988). Assessment in early childhood special education: A typology of dependent measures. In S. M. Odom & K. B. Karnes (Eds.), *Early intervention for infants and children with handicaps* (pp. 23–49). Baltimore: Paul H. Brookes.

Nicolson, S., & Shipstead, S. G. (1994). *Through the looking glass: Observations in the early childhood classroom.* New York: Macmillan.

O'Leary, K. D., & O'Leary, S. (1972). *Classroom management: The successful use of behavior modification.* New York: Pergamon Press.

Page, T. J., & Iwata, B. A. (1986). Interobserver agreement: History, theory, and current methods. In A. Poling & R. W. Fuga (Eds.), *Research methods in applied behavior analysis* (pp. 99–126). New York: Plenum.

Parsons, T., & Bales, R. (1955). *Family socialization and interaction process.* Glencoe, IL: Free Press.

Piaget, J. (1960). *The child's conception of the world.* Patterson, NJ: Littlefield, Adams & Co.

Piaget, J. (1962). *Play, dreams and imitations.* New York: Norton.

Popham, W. J. (Ed.). (1971). *Criterion-referenced measurement.* Englewood Cliffs, NJ: Educational Technology Publications.

Rheingold, H. L. (1982). Ethics as an integral part of research in child development. In R. Vasta (Ed.), *Strategies and techniques of child study* (pp. 305–324). New York: Academic Press.

Rogers-Warren, A. K. (1984). Ecobehavioral analysis. *Education and Treatment of Children, 7,* 283–303.

Rowley, G. L. (1976). The reliability of observational measures. *American Education Research Journal, 13* (1), 51–59.

Rowley, G. L. (1978). The relationship of reliability in classroom research to the amount of observation: An extension of the Spearman-Brown formula. *Journal of Educational Measurement, 15* (3), 165–180.

Russell Sage Foundation. (1969). *Guidelines for the collection, maintenance, and dissemination of pupil records.* New York: Author.

Sattler, J. M. (1988). *Assessment of children's intelligence and special abilities* (3rd ed.). San Diego, CA: Jerome M. Sattler, Publisher.

Scarr, S., Weinberg, R., & Levine, A. (1986). *Understanding development.* San Diego: Harcourt Brace Jovanovich.

Schaefer, C., Gitlin, K., & Sandgrund, A. (Eds.) (1991). *Play diagnosis and assessment.* New York: Wiley.

Schweinhart, L. J. (1993). Observing young children in action: The key to early childhood assessment. *Young Children, 48* (5), 29–33.

Semmel, M. (1975). Application of systematic classroom observation to the study and modification of pupil–teacher interaction in special education. In R. Weinberg & F. Wood (Eds.), *Observation of pupils and teachers in mainstream and special education settings: Alternative strategies* (pp. 231–264). Minneapolis: U.S.O.E. Leadership Institute/Special Education.

Shapiro, E. S. (1987). *Behavioral assessment in school psychology.* Hillsdale, NJ: Lawrence Erlbaum Associates.

Shapiro, E. S., & Skinner, C. H. (1990). Best practices in observation and ecological assessment. In A. Thomas & J. Grimes (Eds.), *Best practices in school psychology–II* (pp. 507–518). Washington, DC: National Association of School Psychologists.

Shepard, L. A. (1994, November). The challenges of assessing young children appropriately. *Phi Delta Kappan,* pp. 206–212.

Sheridan, M. K., Foley, G. M., & Radlinski, S. H. (1995). *Using the supportive play model: Individualized intervention in early childhood practice.* New York: Teachers College Press.

Shinn, M., Rosenfield, S., & Knutson, M. (1989). Varying the difficulty of testing materials: Implications for curriculum-based measurement. *Journal of Special Education, 23* (2), 223–233.

Simon, A., & Boyer, E. G. (Eds.). (1967, 1970). *Mirrors for behavior: An anthology of classroom observation instruments* (vols. A & B). Philadelphia: Research for Better Schools.

Simon, A., & Boyer, E. G. (1969). Technical tools for teaching. In M. Gottsegen & G. Gottsegen (Eds.), *Professional school psychology* (pp. 107–147). New York: Grune & Stratton.

Simon, A., & Boyer, E. G. (Eds.). (1974). *Mirrors for behavior III.* Wyncote, PA: Communications Materials Center.

Smith, P. K., & Connolly, K. J. (1980). *The ecology of preschool behavior.* Cambridge, England: Cambridge University Press.

Society for Research in Child Development. (1982, Winter). Ethical standards for research with children. *Newsletter,* pp. 3–5.

Sparrow, S. S., Balla, D. A., & Cichetti, D. V. (1984). *Vineland adaptive behavior scales.* Circle Pines, MN: American Guidance Service.

Stallings, J. A. (1977). *Learning to look.* Belmont, CA: Wadsworth.

Taplin, P. S., & Reid, J. B. (1973). Effects of instructional set and experimenter influence on observer reliability. *Child Development, 44,* 547–554.

Teale, W. H. (1990). The promise and challenge of informal assessment in early literacy. In L. M. Morrow & J. K. Smith (Eds.), *Assessment for instruction in early literacy* (pp. 45–61). Englewood Cliffs, NJ: Prentice-Hall.

Thorndike, R. L., & Hagen, E. P. (1977). *Measurement and evaluation in psychology and education* (4th ed.). New York: Wiley.

Vasta, R. (1979). *Studying children.* San Francisco: W.H. Freeman & Co.

Vygotsky, L. S. (1978). *Mind in society: The development of higher psychological processes.* Cambridge, MA: Harvard University Press.

Waters, V. (1973). *Teacher differentiated approval and disapproval of boys and girls in the classroom.* Unpublished doctoral dissertation. Teachers College, Columbia University, New York.

Wechsler, D. (1991). *Wechsler Intelligence Scale for Children—III.* San Antonio, TX: Psychological Corporation.

Weinberg, R. (1983). A case of a misplaced conjunction: Nature or nurture? *Journal of School Psychology, 21,* 9–12.

Weinberg, R. (1989). Intelligence and IQ: Landmark issues and great debates. *American Psychologist, 44,* 98–104.

Werner, E. E., & Smith, R. S. (1992). *Overcoming the odds: High risk children from birth to adulthood.* Ithaca, NY: Cornell University Press.

White, B., Watts, J., Barnett, I., Kaban, B., Marmor, J., & Shapiro, B. (1973). *Environment and experience: Major influences on the development of the young child.* Englewood Cliffs, NJ: Prentice-Hall.

White, M. A. (1975). Natural rates of teacher approval and disapproval in the classroom. *Journal of Applied Behavior Analysis, 8,* 367–372.

White, M. A., Beecher, R., Heller, M., & Waters, V. (1973). *Teacher approval/ disapproval record.* New York: Teachers College, Columbia University.

Whitehurst, G. J., Epstein, J. N., Angell, A. L., Payne, A. C., Crone, D. A., & Fischel, J. E. (1994). Outcomes of an emergent literacy intervention in Head Start. *Journal of Educational Psychology, 86,* 542–555.

Wolery, M. (1989). Using direct observation in assessment. In D. B. Bailey & M. Wolery (Eds.), *Assessing infants and preschoolers with handicaps* (pp. 64–96). Columbus, OH: Merrill.

Wright, H. F. (1960). Observational child study. In P. H. Mussen (Ed.), *Handbook of research methods in child development.* New York: Wiley.

Wright, H. F. (1967). *Recording and analyzing child behavior.* New York: Harper & Row.

Wright, L., & Borland, J. H. (1993). Using early childhood developmental portfolios in the identification and education of young, economically disadvantaged, potentially gifted students. *Roeper Review, 15,* 205–210.

Ysseldyke, J. E., & Christenson, S. L. (1993). *The Instructional Environment System–II (TIES–II).* Longmont, CO: Sopris-West.

Ysseldyke, J. E., Christenson, S., & Kovaleski, J. F. (1994). Identifying students' instructional needs in the context of classroom and home environments. *Teaching Exceptional Children, 26* (3), 37–41.

Ysseldyke, J. E., Christenson, S. L., & Thurlow, M. L. (1987). Factors that influence student achievement: An integrative review. *Remedial and Special Education, 10* (5), 21–31.

Bibliography

This bibliography includes general references on the development of observation skills as well as selected observation schedules and systems for observation and recording. Citations already listed in the References are not included in the Bibliography.

Abbott-Shim, M., & Sibley, A. (1987). *Assessment profile for early childhood programs: Manual for administration.* Atlanta: Quality Assist.

Achenbach, T. M., & Edelbrock, C. (1983). *Manual for the Child Behavior Checklist and Revised Child Behavior Profile.* Burlington: Department of Psychiatry, University of Vermont.

Alberto, P. A., & Troutman, A. C. (1982). *Applied behavior analysis for teachers: Influencing student performance.* Columbus, OH: Merrill.

Alberto, P. A., & Troutman, A. C. (1990). *Applied behavior analysis for teachers.* Columbus, OH: Merrill/Macmillan.

Baldwin, C. P. (1965). Naturalistic studies of classroom learning. *Review of Educational Research, 35,* 107–113.

Bales, R. F. (1951). *Interaction process analysis.* Reading, MA: Addison-Wesley.

Barker, R. G. (Ed.). (1963). *The stream of behavior.* New York: Appleton-Century-Crofts.

Becker, W. C., Engelmann, S., & Thomas, D. R. (1975). *Teaching 1: Classroom management.* Chicago: Science Research Associates.

Bell, R. (1964). Structuring parent–child interaction situations for direct observation. *Child Development, 35,* 1009–1020.

Bellack, A. (Ed.). (1963). *Theory and research in teaching.* New York: Teachers College Press.

Bellack, A. S., & Hersen, M. (1988). *Behavioral assessment: A practical handbook* (3rd ed.). New York: Pergamon.

Bergan, J. R., & Feld, J. K. (1993). Developmental assessment: New directions. *Young Children, 48* (5), 41–47.

Biber, B., Murphy, L., Woodcock, L., & Black, I. (1942). *Child life in school: A study of a seven year old group.* New York: Dutton.

Biddle, B. J. (1967). Methods and concepts in classroom research. *Review of Educational Research, 37,* 337–357.

Blurton-Jones, N. A. (Ed.). (1972). *Ethological studies of child behavior.* London: Cambridge University Press.

Coller, A. R. (1972). *Systems for the observation of classroom behavior in early childhood education.* Urbana, IL: ERIC Clearinghouse on Early Childhood Education.

Combs, A. W. (1965). *The professional education of teachers.* Boston: Allyn & Bacon.

Cone, J. D., & Hoier, T. S. (1986). Assessing children: The radical behavioral perspective. In R. J. Prinz (Ed.), *Advances in behavioral assessment of children and families* (vol. 2, pp. 1–27). Greenwich, CT: JAI Press.

Cooper, J. O., Heron, T. E., & Heward, W. L. (1987). *Applied behavior analysis.* Columbus, OH: Merrill/Macmillan.

Deno, S. L., & Fuchs, L. S. (1987). Developing curriculum-based measurement systems for data-based special education problem solving. *Focus on Exceptional Children, 19* (8), 1–16.

Evans, E. D. (1974). Measurement practices in early childhood education. In R. Colvin & E. Zaffiro (Eds.), *Preschool education: A handbook for the training of early childhood educators.* New York: Springer.

Eyberg, S. M., & Robinson, E. A. (1983). Dyadic parent–child interaction coding system: A manual. *Psychological Documents, 13* (MS. No. 2582).

Feagans, L. (1972). Ecological theory as a model for constructing a theory of emotional disturbance. In W. C. Rhodes & M. L. Tracy (Eds.), *A study of child variance, Vol. 1: Conceptual models* (pp. 323–389). Ann Arbor, MI: Institute for the Study of Mental Retardation and Related Disabilities.

Fine, G. A., & Sandstrom, K. L. (1988). *Knowing children: Participant observation with children.* Newbury Park, CA: Sage.

Foster, S. L., Bell-Dolan, D. J., & Burge, D. A. (1988). Behavioral observation. In A. S. Bellack & M. Hersen (Eds.), *Behavioral assessment: A practical handbook.* New York: Pergamon.

Gagné, R. M. (1973). Observations of school learning. *Educational Psychologist, 10,* 112–116.

Gallagher, J. A., Nuthall, G., & Rosenshine, B. (1970). *Classroom observation* (AERA Monograph Series on Curriculum Evaluation). Chicago: Rand McNally.

Garbarino, J. (1982). *Children and families in the social environment.* New York: Aldine.

Gellert, E. (1955). Systematic observation: A method of child study. *Harvard Educational Review, 25,* 179–195.

Genishi, C. (1982). Observational research methods for early childhood education. In B. Spodek (Ed.), *Handbook of research in early childhood education* (pp. 564–591). New York: Free Press.

Genishi, C. (1992). Individuals, observations and study of. In L. Williams & D. Fromberg (Eds.), *Encyclopedia of early childhood education* (pp. 625–670). New York: Garland.

Goodenough, F. (1937). The observation of children's behavior as a method in social psychology. *Social Forces, 15,* 476–479.

Goodwin, W. L., & Driscoll, L. A. (1980). *Handbook for measurement and evaluation in early childhood education.* San Francisco: Jossey-Bass.

Gordon, I. (1966). *Studying the child in school.* New York: Wiley.

Hammill, D. D., & Bartel, N. R. (1982). *Teaching children with learning and behavior problems.* Boston: Allyn & Bacon.

Herbert, J. (1970). Observations as a research technique. *Psychology in the Schools, 1,* 124–135.

Herbert, J. O., & Attridge, C. (1975). A guide for developers and users of observation systems and manuals. *American Educational Research Journal, 12,* 1–20.

Hersen, M., & Bellack, A. S. (1981). *Behavioral assessment: A practical handbook* (2nd ed.). New York: Pergamon.

Heyns, R. W., & Lippitt, R. (1954). Systematic observation techniques. In G. Lindzey (Ed.), *Handbook of social psychology, Vol. 1: Theory and method* (pp. 370–404). Cambridge, MA: Addison-Wesley.

High/Scope Educational Research Foundation. (1992a). *High/Scope observation record (COR) for ages 2½–6.* Ypsilanti, MI: High/Scope Press.

High/Scope Educational Research Foundation. (1992b). *Teacher's manual.* Ypsilanti, MI: High/Scope Press.

Hutt, S. J., & Hutt, C. (1970). *Direct observation and measurement of behavior.* Springfield, IL: Thomas.

Jersild, A. T., & Meigs, M. F. (1939). Direct observation as a research method. *Review of Education Research, 9,* 472–482.

Jones, R. R., Reid, J. B., & Patterson, G. R. (1975). Naturalistic observation in clinical assessment. In P. McReynolds (Ed.), *Advances in psychological assessment* (vol. 3, pp. 42–95). San Francisco: Jossey-Bass.

Kazdin, A. E. (1980). *Behavior modification in applied settings* (Rev. ed.). Homewood, IL: Dorsey.

Kazdin, A. E. (1989). *Behavior modification in applied settings.* Pacific Grove, CA: Brooks/Cole Publishing.

Kerr, M. M., & Nelson, C. M. (1989). *Strategies for managing behavior problems in the classroom* (2nd ed.). Columbus, OH: Merrill/Macmillan.

Koorland, M. A., Monda, L. E., & Vail, C. O. (1988). Recording behavior with ease. *Teaching Exceptional Children, 21,* 59–61.

Lambert, N. M., Cox, H. W., & Hartsough, C. S. (1970). The observability of intellectual functioning of first graders. *Psychology in the Schools, 7,* 74–85.

Lennox, D. B., & Miltenberger, R. G. (1989). Conducting a functional assessment of problem behavior in applied setting. *The Journal of the Association for Persons with Severe Handicaps, 14,* 304–311.

Lewin, K. (1951). Psychological ecology. In D. Cartwright (Ed.), *Field theory in social science: Selected theoretical papers by Kurt Lewin* (pp. 170–187). New York: Harper & Row.

Lynch, W. W. (1977). Guidelines to the use of classroom observation instruments by school psychologists. *School Psychology Monograph, 3* (1), 1–22.

Mattick, I., & Perkin, F. J. (1973). *Guidelines for observation and assessment: An approach to evaluating a learning environment of a daycare center.* Washington, DC: Daycare and Child Development Council of America.

McConnell, S. R., & Odom, S. L. (1987). Sociometric measures. In *Dictionary of behavioral assessment techniques* (pp. 432–434). Elmsburg, NY: Pergamon.

Medinnus, R. (1976). *Child study and observation guide.* New York: Wiley.

Mehrabian, A. (1969). Some referents and measures of non-verbal behavior. *Behavior Research Methods and Instrumentation, 1,* 203–207.

Melbin, M. (1954). Field methods and techniques: An interaction recording device for participant observers. *Human Organization, 13,* 29–33.

Miller, D. (1979). Role of naturalistic observation in comparative psychology. *American Psychologist, 32,* 211–219.

Minnesota Department of Education, Special Education Section. (1980). *A consideration of the assessment process for handicapped children under five: Observing the behavior of young children and assessing the environments in which they learn.* St. Paul: Minnesota Department of Education.

Moos, R. H. (1973). Conceptualizations of human environments. *American Psychologist, 23,* 652–665.

Morine, G. (1975). Interaction analysis in the classroom: Alternative applications. In R. Weinberg & F. Wood (Eds.), *Observation of pupils and teachers in mainstream and special education settings: Alternative strategies* (pp. 75–95). Minneapolis: U.S.O.E. Leadership Training Institute/Special Education.

Morris, R. J. (1985). *Behavior modification with exceptional children.* Glenview, IL: Scott, Foresman.

Openshaw, M. K., & Cyphert, F. (1966). *Development of a taxonomy for the classification of teacher classroom behavior* (Taxonomy of Teacher Behavior). Columbus: OH: State University Research Foundation.

Paget, K. D., & Bracken, B. A. (Eds.). (1982). *The psychoeducational assessment of preschool children.* New York: Grune & Stratton.

Patterson, G. R. (1976). *Living with children: New methods for parents and teachers.* Champaign, IL: Research Press.

Perkins, H. (1964). A procedure for assessing the classroom behavior of students and teachers. *American Educational Research Journal, 1,* 249–260.

Randhawa, B. S., & Fu, L. W. (1973). Assessment and effect of some classroom environment variables. *Review of Educational Research, 43,* 303–322.

Resnick, L. B. (1976). Task analysis in instructional design: Some cases from mathematics. In D. Klahr (Ed.), *Cognition and instruction* (pp. 51–80). Hillsdale, NJ: Erlbaum.

Riskin, J. (1964). Family interaction scales: A preliminary report. *Archives of General Psychiatry, 11,* 484–494.

Rosenshine, B., & Furst, N. (1973). The use of direct observation to study learning. In R. M. W. Travers (Ed.), *Second handbook of research on teaching* (pp. 122–183). Chicago: Rand McNally.

Rowen, B. J. (1973). *The children we see: An observational approach to child study.* New York: Holt, Rinehart & Winston.

Rutter, M. A. (1967). A children's behavior questionnaire for completion by teachers: Preliminary findings. *Journal of Child Psychology and Psychiatry, 8,* 1–11.

Ryans, D. (1960). *Characteristics of teachers.* Washington, DC: American Council on Education.

Sackett, G. P. (Ed.). (1978). *Observing behavior* (2 vols.). Baltimore: University Park Press.

Scarr, S., & Weinberg, R. (1986). The early childhood enterprise: Care and education of the young. *American Psychologist, 41,* 140–146.

Schalock, H. D., & Hale, J. (Eds.). (1968). *A competency based, field-centered systems approach to elementary teacher education, Vol. 1: Overview and specifications.* Portland, OH: Northwest Regional Educational Research Laboratory.

Semmel, M., & Thiagarajan, S. (1973). Observation systems and the special education teacher. *Focus on Exceptional Children, 5,* 1–12.

Shapiro, E. S. (1987). *Behavioral assessment in school psychology.* Hillsdale, NJ: Lawrence Erlbaum Associates.

Shapiro, E. S., & Lentz, F. E. (1986). Behavioral assessment of academic behavior. In T. R. Kratochwill (Ed.), *Advances in school psychology* (vol. 5, pp. 87–139). Hillsdale, NJ: Lawrence Erlbaum Associates.

Shure, M. B. (1963). Psychological ecology of a nursery school. *Child Development, 34,* 979–992.

Simon, A., & Agazarian, Y. (1967). *Sequel analysis of verbal interaction (SAVI).* Philadelphia: Research for Better Schools.

Soar, R. S., Soar, R. M., & Ragosta, M. (1971). *The Florida climate and control system (FLACCS).* Gainesville: Institute for Development of Human Resources, College of Education, University of Florida.

Spaulding, R. (1967a). (Coping Analysis Schedule for Educational Settings [CASES]). *An introduction to the use of the coping analysis schedule for educational settings and S-T-A-R-S.* Durham, NC: Education Improvement Program, Duke University.

Spaulding, R. (1967b). (Spaulding Teacher Activity Rating Schedule [STARS]). *An introduction to the use of C-A-S-E-S and STARS.* Durham, NC: Education Improvement Program, Duke University.

Spindler, G. (1982). *Doing the ethnography of schooling: Educational anthropology in action.* New York: Holt, Rinehart & Winston.

Thurman, S. K., & Widerstrom, A. H. (1985). *Young children with special needs: A developmental and ecological approach.* Boston: Allyn & Bacon.

Walsh, D. J., Tobin, J., Joseph, J., & Grave, M. E. (1993). The interpretative voice: Qualitative research in early childhood education. In B. Spodek (Ed.), *Handbook of research on the education of young children* (pp. 464–476). New York: Macmillan.

Weick, K. (1968). Systematic observation methods. In G. Lindzey & E. Aronson (Eds.), *Handbook of social psychology, Vol. 2: Research methods* (pp. 357–451). Reading, MA: Addison-Wesley.

Weinberg, R., & Wood, F. (Eds.). (1975). *Observation of pupils and teachers in mainstream and special education settings: Alternative strategies.* Minneapolis: U.S.O.E. Leadership Training Institute/Special Education.

Westbury, I., & Bellack, A. (Eds.). (1971). *Research into classroom processes.* New York: Teachers College Press.

White, O. R., & Haring, N. G. (1980). *Exceptional teaching.* Columbus, OH: Merrill.

Willems, P., & Raush, H. L. (Eds.). (1968). *Naturalistic viewpoints in psychological research.* New York: Holt, Rinehart & Winston.

Withall, J. (1960). Observing and recording behavior. *Review of Educational Research, 30,* 496–512.

Withall, J. (1969). Evaluation of classroom climate. *Childhood Education, 45,* 403–408.

Wrightstone, J. W. (1960). Observational techniques. In C. W. Harris & M. R. Liba (Eds.), *Encyclopedia of educational research* (3rd ed., pp. 927–933). New York: Macmillan.

Zirpoli, T., & Melloy, K. (1993). *Behavior management.* New York: Merrill/Macmillan.

Index

About the Authors

Ann E. Boehm, Ph.D., is Professor of Psychology and Education at Teachers College, Columbia University. Her scholarly interests center on preschool and child assessment, concept acquisition in young children, early reading, and intergenerational literacy. She is the author of the *Boehm Test of Basic Concepts (Revised)*, *Boehm Resource Guide for Basic Concept Teaching*, and co-author of the *Cognitive Skills Assessment Battery*. Boehm is past chair of the Department of Developmental and Educational Psychology.

Richard A. Weinberg, Ph.D., the Birkmaier Professor of Educational Leadership, is a Professor of Child Psychology and Adjunct Professor of Psychology and Educational Psychology at the University of Minnesota–Twin Cities, where he is Director of the Institute of Child Development. Dr. Weinberg's scholarship focuses on the study of individual differences in the development of intelligence and personality characteristics and on the assessment of young children. He has co-authored or edited several other books, has served on the Professional Advisory Board of *Baby Talk Magazine*, and is editor of *Applied Developmental Science*. Weinberg currently chairs a National Advisory Board for a new TV series for parent being developed by PBS.